TOWARD THE
AFRICAN
REVOLUTION

—*Political Essays*—

Works by Frantz Fanon
Published by Grove Press

BLACK SKIN, WHITE MASKS
A DYING COLONIALISM
TOWARD THE AFRICAN REVOLUTION
THE WRETCHED OF THE EARTH

TOWARD THE AFRICAN REVOLUTION

—Political Essays—

FRANTZ FANON

translated from the French by
HAAKON CHEVALIER

GROVE PRESS
New York

First published in France under the title Pour la Révolution Africaine

Published simultaneously in Canada

Printed in the United States of America

Library of Congress Cataloging-in-Publication Data

Fanon, Frantz, 1925–1961.
    Toward the African revolution.

    Translation of: Pour la révolution africaine.
    1. Africa—Politics and government—1945–1960.
2. Algeria—Politics and government—1945–1960.
I. Title.
DT30.2.F3613   1988   320.5'092'4   87-37247
ISBN 978-0-8021-3090-7

Grove Press
an imprint of Grove Atlantic
154 West 14th Street
New York, NY 10011

Distributed by Publishers Group West

groveatlantic.com

21 22 23 24 25   15 14 13 12 11

Contents

v

Editorial Note

The political essays, articles, and notes by Frantz Fanon published in the present volume cover the most active period of his life, from the publication of *Peau Noir, Masques Blancs* [*Black Skin, White Masks*] in 1952—he was then twenty-eight years old —to that of *Les Damnés de la Terre* [*The Wretched of the Earth*] in 1961 which was to coincide, within a matter of days, with the date of his death.

Most of these writings have already appeared in various reviews and periodicals, the reference and the date of which we give in each case. But they were widely scattered and difficult to get hold of. Those that appeared in *El Moudjahid,* in particular, are hardly to be found today, and they had in fact been accessible, when they appeared, only to a limited number of readers.

Brought together as they are here, in their chronological order, these writings reveal a singularly living unity. They mark the successive stages of a single combat, which develops and broadens, but the objective and the means of which had been seen and determined from the beginning. The three books so far published give us three analyses crystallized at precise stages of Fanon's development. The texts that follow constitute a guiding thread by which we may follow him more closely from day to day, the itinerary of a mind in constant evolution, growing ever broader and richer while continuing to be true to itself.

The first two articles, "The North-African Syndrome" and "West Indians and Africans," published in 1952 and 1955, may mark the first stages. At this time Frantz Fanon had completed his psychiatric studies: he was thus in a position, on the basis of his daily medical experience, to give a scientific account of the situation of the colonized. On the other hand this situation was one that he had lived historically, that he was still living; it was for him a personal experience which he could judge from within as well. Having decided to dissociate himself both from the "great white error" and from the "great black mirage," he initiated a new, revolutionary approach. To present the question of the colonized and to solve it, he was in a privileged position: his consciousness of it, the clarity of his vision, strengthened the firmness of his commitment.

Fanon was to choose to practice in Algeria, an outstandingly colonialist country, to live and fight among other colonized people like himself. The theme is taken up again and amplified in "Racism and Culture," a lecture delivered in 1956 before the First Congress of Negro Writers. Here the analysis becomes sharper, the challenge radical, the commitment open and precise. His diagnosis of racism which "is not an accidental discovery" but "fits into a definite pattern, which is the pattern of the exploitation of one group of men by another," implies one solution and one only: "The logical end of this will to fight is the total liberation of the national territory." "The struggle has suddenly become total, absolute." This is not a verbal struggle. From the time he became a psychiatrist at the Blida hospital, and even more after the outbreak of the insurrection, Fanon was a militant in the Algerian revolutionary organization. At the same time he carried on a remarkable medical activity, innovating at many levels, deeply, viscerally close to his patients whom he regarded as primarily victims of the system he was fighting. He collected clinical notes and analyses on the phenomena of colonialist alienation seen through mental diseases. He explored local traditions and their relations to colonization. This material remains untouched, but it too is scattered, and we hope to be able to assemble it and present it in a separate volume.

His work as an FLN [National Liberation Front] militant soon attracted the attention of the French police. Late in 1956, before leaving for Tunis, he made final a much older total commitment through his letter of resignation, "Letter to the Resident Minister." It is, together with the "Letter to a Frenchman," hitherto unpublished, the only piece of writing that bears witness to this period; the two letters form the chapter, "For Algeria." The experience thus accumulated in the very thick of the battle was later to furnish the material for *L'An Cinq de la Révolution Algérienne,* published in 1959.*

In Tunis, Fanon was called upon to participate in the Press Services of the FLN. He was one of the team of editors of *El Moudjahid* of which the first issues then appeared. Relentlessly he lashed out at the colonialist system, its total nature, its unbroken unity, the solidarity which, whether they willed it or not, bound those that were on its side, while at the same time the genocide of one million Algerians was being carried out. His analysis, "French Intellectuals and Democrats and the Algerian Revolution," aroused the indignation of the French Left. In it he denounced the hypocrisy of those who considered colonialism and its sequels, war, torture, as only a monstrous excrescence which had only to be circumscribed and reproved, whereas it was really a perfectly logical, perfectly coherent whole, in which all those who lived within it were inevitably accomplices.

Fanon had thus grasped the means of amplifying one of his first themes: the common nature of the struggle of all the colonized. Being one of the first to envisage concretely—not as a "prophetic vision" but as an immediate battle objective—the unity of Africa, he was constantly linking the fate of the Algerian Revolution with that of the continent as a whole, considering it, as he did, the vanguard of the African Revolution. *El Moudjahid* constantly developed this line: *The Algerian Revolution and the Liberation of Africa*—this title given to a booklet of FLN articles and documents widely distributed at this period well indicates the importance that the Algerian revolutionaries then attributed to it.

The articles in *El Moudjahid* were never signed. The anonymity was complete. The articles published here, checked

* Published in the United States in 1965 under the title, *Studies in a Dying Colonialism.*

by Mrs. Fanon, are those we are absolutely certain were written by Fanon. His contribution, to be sure, was not limited to these particular articles. But as in every team, and particularly in this revolution in full ferment, there was constant osmosis, interaction, mutual stimulation. At the very time when Fanon's thinking was reaching new dimensions in contact with the creative nucleus of the Algerian Revolution, it would transmit new impulses to the latter. We have assembled the texts thus produced under the title, "Toward the Liberation of Africa."

The idea of Africa that was growing in Fanon's mind found concrete expression in the mission that he conducted in the countries of West Africa, after having been ambassador at Accra. He was to study, in particular, the conditions of a closer alliance between Africans, the recruiting of Negro volunteers, the opening of a new front South of the Sahara. The pages that we publish in the last chapter, "African Unity," are those of an unpublished travel notebook in which this plan assumes its full clarity and its violence.

Fanon returned from this mission exhausted: he had contracted leukemia. He devoted his last strength to writing *Les Damnés de la Terre*. He was to die a year after having witnessed the fall of his friend, Lumumba, the African leader whose African vision was closest to his. He believed steadfastly in the forthcoming total liberation of Africa, convinced, as he had written in *L'An Cinq de la Révolution Algerienne*, that the African revolution had created "an irreversible situation."

FRANÇOIS MASPERO

Paris, 1964

I

The Problem of the Colonized

1

The "North African Syndrome"

It is a common saying that man is constantly a challenge to himself, and that were he to claim that he is so no longer he would be denying himself. It must be possible, however, to describe an initial, a basic dimension of all human problems. More precisely, it would seem that all the problems which man faces on the subject of man can be reduced to this one question:

"Have I not, because of what I have done or failed to do, contributed to an impoverishment of human reality?"

The question could also be formulated in this way:

"Have I at all times demanded and brought out the man that is in me?"

I want to show in what is to follow that, in the specific case of the North African who has emigrated to France, a theory of inhumanity is in a fair way to finding its laws and its corollaries.

All those men who are hungry, all those men who are cold, all those men who are afraid . . .

All those men of whom *we* are afraid, who crush the jealous emerald of our dreams, who twist the fragile curve of our smiles, all those men we face, who ask us no questions, but to whom we put strange ones.

Who are they?

I ask you, I ask myself. Who are they, those creatures starving for humanity who stand buttressed against the impalpable frontiers (though I know them from experience to be terribly distinct) of complete recognition?

Who are they, in truth, those creatures, who hide, who are

First published in *L'Esprit*, February, 1952.

hidden by social truth beneath the attributes of *bicot, bou-nioule, arabe, raton, sidi, mon z'ami?*[1]

FIRST THESIS.—*That the behavior of the North African often causes a medical staff to have misgivings as to the reality of his illness.*

Except in urgent cases—an intestinal occlusion, wounds, ac-cidents—the North African arrives enveloped in vagueness.

He has an ache in his belly, in his back, he has an ache every-where. He suffers miserably, his face is eloquent, he is obviously suffering.

"What's wrong, my friend?"

"I'm dying, *monsieur le docteur.*"

His voice breaks imperceptibly.

"Where do you have pain?"

"Everywhere, *monsieur le docteur.*"

You must not ask for specific symptoms: you would not be given any. For example, in pains of an ulcerous character, it is important to know their periodicity. This conformity to the categories of time is something to which the North African seems to be hostile. It is not lack of comprehension, for he often comes accompanied by an interpreter. It is as though it is an effort for him to go back to where he no longer is. The past for him is a burning past. What he hopes is that he will never suffer again, never again be face to face with that past. This present pain, which visibly mobilizes the muscles of his face, suffices him. He does not understand that anyone should wish to im-pose on him, even by way of memory, the pain that is already gone. He does not understand why the doctor asks him so many questions.

"Where does it hurt?"

"In my belly." (He then points to his thorax and abdomen.)

"When does it hurt?"

"All the time."

"Even at night?"

[1] Terms of contempt applied in France to Arabs in general and to Algerians in particular.—*Tr.*

"Especially at night."

"It hurts more at night than in the daytime, does it?"

"No, all the time."

"But more at night than in the daytime?"

"No, all the time."

"And where does it hurt most?"

"Here." (He then points to his thorax and abdomen.)

And there you are. Meanwhile patients are waiting outside, and the worst of it is that you have the impression that time would not improve matters. You therefore fall back on a diagnosis of probability and in correlation propose an approximate therapy.

"Take this treatment for a month. If you don't get better, come back and see me."

There are then two possibilities:

1. The patient is not immediately relieved, and he comes back after three or four days. This sets us against him, because we know that it takes time for the prescribed medicine to have an effect on the lesion. He is made to understand this, or more precisely, he is told. But our patient has not heard what we said. He *is* his pain and he refuses to understand any language, and it is not far from this to the conclusion: It is because I am Arab that they don't treat me like others.

2. The patient is not immediately relieved, but he does not go back to the same doctor, nor to the same dispensary. He goes elsewhere. He proceeds on the assumption that in order to get satisfaction he has to knock at every door, and he knocks. He knocks persistently. Gently. Naïvely. Furiously.

He knocks. The door is opened. The door is always opened. And he tells about *his pain*. Which becomes increasingly his own. He now talks about it volubly. He takes hold of it in space and puts it before the doctor's nose. He takes it, touches it with his ten fingers, develops it, exposes it. It grows as one watches it. He gathers it over the whole surface of his body and after fifteen minutes of gestured explanations the interpreter (appropriately baffling) translates for us: he says he has a belly-ache.

All those forays into space, all those facial spasms, all those wild stares were only meant to express a vague discomfort. We experience a kind of frustration in the field of explanation. The comedy, or the drama, begins all over again: approximate diagnosis and therapy.

There is no reason for the wheel to stop going round. Some day an X-ray will be taken of him which will show an ulcer or a gastritis. Or which in most cases will show nothing at all. His ailment will be described as "functional."

This concept is of some importance and is worth looking into. A thing is said to be vague when it is lacking in consistency, in objective reality. The North African's pain, for which we can find no lesional basis, is judged to have no consistency, no reality. Now the North African *is* a-man-who-doesn't-like-work. So that whatever he does will be interpreted *a priori* on the basis of this.

A North African is hospitalized because he suffers from lassitude, asthenia, weakness. He is given active treatment on the basis of restoratives. After twenty days it is decided to discharge him. He then discovers that he has another disease.

"My heart seems to flutter inside here."

"My head is bursting."

In the face of this fear of leaving the hospital one begins to wonder if the debility for which he was treated was not due to some giddiness. One begins to wonder if one has not been the plaything of this patient whom one has never too well understood. Suspicion rears its head. Henceforth one will mistrust the alleged symptoms.

The thing is perfectly clear in the winter; so much so that certain wards are literally submerged by North Africans during the severe cold spells. It's so comfortable within hospital walls.

In one ward, a doctor was scolding a European suffering from sciatica who spent the day visiting in the different rooms. The doctor explained to him that with his particular ailment, rest constituted one half of the therapy. With the North Africans, he added, for our benefit, the problem is different: there is no need to prescribe rest; they're always in bed.

In the face of this pain without lesion, this illness distributed in and over the whole body, this continuous suffering, the easiest attitude, to which one comes more or less rapidly, is the negation of any morbidity. When you come down to it, the North African is a simulator, a liar, a malingerer, a sluggard, a thief.[2]

SECOND THESIS.—*That the attitude of medical personnel is very often an* a priori *attitude. The North African does not come with a substratum common to his race, but on a foundation built by the European. In other words, the North African, spontaneously, by the very fact of appearing on the scene, enters into a pre-existing framework.*

For several years medicine has shown a trend which, in a very summary way, we can call neo-Hippocratism. In accordance with this trend doctors, when faced with a patient, are concerned less with making a diagnosis of an organ than with a diagnosis of a function. But this orientation has not yet found favor in the medical schools where pathology is taught. There is a flaw in the practitioner's thinking. An extremely dangerous flaw.

We shall see how it manifests itself in practice.

I am called in to visit a patient on an emergency. It is two o'clock in the morning. The room is dirty, the patient is dirty. His parents are dirty. Everybody weeps. Everybody screams. One has the strange impression that death is hovering nearby. The young doctor does not let himself be perturbed. He "objectively" examines the belly that has every appearance of requiring surgery.

He touches, he feels, he taps, he questions, but he gets only groans by way of response. He feels again, taps a second time, and the belly contracts, resists. . . . He "sees nothing." But what if an operation is really called for? What if he is overlooking something? His examination is negative, but he doesn't dare to leave. After considerable hesitation, he will send his patient to a center with the diagnosis of an abdomen requiring surgery. Three days later he sees the patient with the "abdomen requiring surgery" turn up smilingly in his office, completely

[2] *Social Security? It's we who pay for it!*

cured. And what the patient is unaware of is that there is an exacting medical philosophy, and that he has flouted this philosophy.

Medical thinking proceeds from the symptom to the lesion. In the illustrious assemblies, in the international medical congresses, agreement has been reached as to the importance of the neurovegetative systems, the diencephalon, the endocrine glands, the psychosomatic links, the sympathalgias, but doctors continue to be taught that every symptom requires its lesion. The patient who complains of headaches, ringing in his ears, and dizziness, will also have high blood-pressure. But should it happen that along with these symptoms there is no sign of high blood-pressure, nor of brain tumor, in any case nothing positive, the doctor would have to conclude that medical thinking was at fault; and as any thinking is necessarily thinking about something, he will find the *patient* at fault—an indocile, undisciplined patient, who doesn't know the rules of the game. Especially the rule, known to be inflexible, which says: any symptom presupposes a lesion.

What am I to do with this patient? From the specialist to whom I had sent him for a probable operation, he comes back to me with a diagnosis of "North African syndrome." And it is true that the newly arrived medico will run into situations reminiscent of Molière through the North Africans he is called upon to treat. A man who fancies himself to be ill! If Molière (what I am about to say is utterly stupid, but all these lines only explicate, only make more flagrant, something vastly more stupid), if Molière had had the privilege of living in the twentieth century, he would certainly not have written *Le Malade Imaginaire*, for there can be no doubt that Argan is ill, is actively ill:

"*Comment, coquine! Si je suis malade! Si je suis malade, impudente!*"[3]

The North African syndrome. The North African today who goes to see a doctor bears the dead weight of all his compatriots.

[3] "What, you hussy! you doubt if I'm sick! You doubt if I'm sick, you impudent wench!"

Of all those who had only symptoms, of all those about whom the doctors said, "Nothing you can put your teeth into." (Meaning: no lesion.) But the patient who is here, in front of me, this body which I am forced to assume to be swept by a consciousness, this body which is no longer altogether a body or rather which is doubly a body since it is beside itself with terror —this body which asks me to listen to it without, however, paying too much heed to it—fills me with exasperation.

"Where do you hurt?"

"In my stomach." (He points to his liver.)

I lose my patience. I tell him that the stomach is to the left, that what he is pointing to is the location of the liver. He is not put out, he passes the palm of his hand over that mysterious belly.

"It all hurts."

I happen to know that this "it all" contains three organs; more exactly five or six. That each organ has *its* pathology. The pathology invented by the Arab does not interest us. It is a pseudo-pathology. The Arab is a pseudo-invalid.

Every Arab is a man who suffers from an imaginary ailment. The young doctor or the young student who has never seen a sick Arab *knows* (the old medical tradition testifies to it) that "those fellows are humbugs." There is one thing that might give food for thought. Speaking to an Arab, the student or the doctor is inclined to use the second person singular. It's a nice thing to do, we are told . . . to put them at ease . . . they're used to it . . . I am sorry, but I find myself incapable of analyzing this phenomenon without departing from the objective attitude to which I have constrained myself.

"I can't help it," an intern once told me, "I can't talk to them in the same way that I talk to other patients."

Yes, to be sure: "I can't help it." If you only knew the things in my life that I can't help. If you only knew the things in my life that plague me during the hours when others are benumbing their brains. If you only knew . . . but you will never know.

The medical staff discovers the existence of a North African

syndrome. Not experimentally, but on the basis of an oral tradition. The North African takes his place in this asymptomatic
syndrome and is automatically put down as undisciplined (cf.
medical discipline), inconsequential (with reference to the law
according to which every symptom implies a lesion), and in-
sincere (he says he is suffering when we know there are no
reasons for suffering). There is a floating idea which is present,
just beyond the limit of my lack of good faith, which emerges
when the Arab unveils himself through his language:

"Doctor, I'm going to die."

This idea, after having passed through a number of contor-
tions, will impose itself, will impose itself on me.

No, you certainly can't take these fellows seriously.

THIRD THESIS.—*That the greatest willingness, the purest of intentions require enlightenment. Concerning the necessity of
making a situational diagnosis.*

Dr. Stern, in an article on psychosomatic medicine, based on
the work of Heinrich Meng, writes: "One must not only find
out which organ is attacked, what is the nature of the organic
lesions, if they exist, and what microbe has invaded the organism; it is not enough to know the 'somatic constitution' of
the patient. One must try to find out what Meng calls his 'situation,' *that is to say, his relations with his associates, his occupations and his preoccupations, his sexuality, his sense of security
or of insecurity, the dangers that threaten him; and we may add
also his evolution, the story of his life. One must make a 'situational diagnosis.'* "[4]

Dr. Stern offers us a magnificent plan, and we shall follow it.

1. *Relations with his associates.* Must we really speak of this?
Is there not something a little comical about speaking of the
North African's relations with his associates, in France? Does he
have relations? Does he *have* associates? Is he not alone? Are
they not alone? Don't they seem absurd to us, that is to say

[4] Dr. E. Stern. "Médecine psychosomatique," *Psyché,* Jan.-Feb. 1949, p. 128.
Emphasis added.

without substance, in the trams and the trolleybuses? Where do they come from? Where are they going? From time to time one sees them working at some building, but one does not *see* them, one perceives them, one gets a glimpse of them. Associates? Relations? There are no contracts. There are only bumps. Do people realize how much that is gentle and polite is contained in this word, "contact"? Are there contacts? Are there relations?

2. *Occupations and preoccupations.* He works, he is busy, he busies himself, he is kept busy. His preoccupations? I think the word does not exist in his language. What would he concern himself with? In France we say: *Il se préoccupe de trouver du travail* (he concerns himself with looking for work); in North Africa: he busies himself looking for work.

"Excuse me, Madame, but in your opinion, what are the preoccupations of a North African?"

3. *Sexuality.* Yes, I know what you mean; it consists of rape. In order to show to what extent a scotomizing study can be prejudicial to the authentic unveiling of a phenomenon, I should like to reproduce a few lines from a doctoral thesis in medicine presented in Lyon in 1951 by Dr. Léon Mugniery:

"In the region of Saint Etienne, eight out of ten have married prostitutes. Most of the others have accidental and short-time mistresses, sometimes on a marital basis. Often they put up one or several prostitutes for a few days and bring their friends in to them.

"*For prostitution seems to play an important role in the North African colony*[5] . . . It is due to the powerful sexual appetite that is characteristic of those hot-blooded southerners."

Further on:

"It can be shown by many examples that attempts made to house North Africans decently have repeatedly failed.

"These are mostly young men (25 to 35) with great sexual needs, whom the bonds of a mixed marriage can only temporarily stabilize, and for whom homosexuality is a disastrous inclination . . .

[5] Emphasis added.

"There are few solutions to this problem: either, in spite of the *risks*[6] involved in a certain invasion by the Arab family, the regrouping of this family in France should be encouraged and Arab girls and women should be brought here; or else houses of prostitution for them should be tolerated . . .

"If these factors are not taken into account, we may well be exposed to increasing attempts at rape, of the kind that the newspapers are constantly reporting. Public morals surely have more to fear from the existence of these facts than from the existence of brothels."

And to conclude, Dr. Mugniery deplores the mistake made by the French government in the following sentence which appears in capitals in his thesis: "THE GRANTING OF FRENCH CITIZENSHIP, CONFERRING EQUALITY OF RIGHTS, SEEMS TO HAVE BEEN TOO HASTY AND BASED ON SENTIMENTAL AND POLITICAL REASONS, RATHER THAN ON THE FACT OF THE SOCIAL AND INTELLECTUAL EVOLUTION OF A RACE HAVING A CIVILIZATION THAT IS AT TIMES REFINED BUT STILL PRIMITIVE IN ITS SOCIAL, FAMILY AND SANITARY BEHAVIOR." (p. 45).

Need anything be added? Should we take up these absurd sentences one after the other? Should we remind Dr. Mugniery that if the North Africans in France content themselves with prostitutes, it is because they find prostitutes here in the first place, and also because they do not find any Arab women (who might invade the nation)?

4. *His inner tension.* Utterly unrealistic! You might as well speak of the inner tension of a stone. Inner tension indeed! What a joke!

5. *His sense of security or of insecurity.* The first term has to be struck out. The North African is in a perpetual state of insecurity. A multisegmented insecurity.

I sometimes wonder if it would not be well to reveal to the average Frenchman that it is a misfortune to be a North African. The North African is never sure. He has rights, you will tell me, but he doesn't know what they are. Ah! Ah! It's up to

[6] Emphasis added.

him to know them. Yes, sure, we're back on our feet! Rights, Duties, Citizenship, Equality, what fine things! The North African on the threshold of the French Nation—which is, we are told, his as well—experiences in the political realm, on the plane of citizenship, an imbroglio which no one is willing to face. What connection does this have with the North African in a hospital setting? It so happens that there *is* a connection.

6. *The dangers that threaten him.* Threatened in his affectivity, threatened in his social activity, threatened in his membership in the community—the North African combines all the conditions that make a sick man.

Without a family, without love, without human relations, without communion with the group, the first encounter with himself will occur in a neurotic mode, in a pathological mode; he will feel himself emptied, without life, in a bodily struggle with death, a death on this side of death, a death in life—and what is more pathetic than this man with robust muscles who tells us in his truly broken voice, "Doctor, I'm going to die"?

7. *His evolution and the story of his life.* It would be better to say the history of his death. A daily death.

A death in the tram,
a death in the doctor's office,
a death with the prostitutes,
a death on the job site,
a death at the movies,
a multiple death in the newspapers,
a death in the fear of all decent folk of going out after midnight.
A death,
yes a DEATH.

All this is very fine, we shall be told, but what solutions do you propose?

As you know, they are vague, amorphous . . .

"You constantly have to be on their backs."

"You've got to push them out of the hospital."

"If you were to listen to them you would prolong their con-
valescence indefinitely."

"They can't express themselves."

And they are liars
and also they are thieves
and also and also and also
the Arab is a thief
all Arabs are thieves
It's a do-nothing race
dirty
disgusting
Nothing you can do about them
nothing you can get out of them
sure, it's hard for them being the way they are
being that way
but anyway, you can't say it's our fault.

—But that's just it, it *is* our fault.

It so happens that the fault is YOUR fault.

Men come and go along a corridor you have built for them,
where you have provided no bench on which they can rest,
where you have crystallized a lot of scarecrows that viciously
smack them in the face, and hurt their cheeks, their chests, their
hearts.

Where they find no room
where you leave them no room
where there is absolutely no room for them
and you dare tell me it doesn't concern you!
that it's no fault of yours!

This man whom you thingify by calling him systematically
Mohammed, whom you reconstruct, or rather whom you dis-
solve, on the basis of an idea, an idea you know to be repulsive
(you know perfectly well you rob him of something, that something for which not so long ago you were ready to give up
everything, even your life) well, don't you have the impression
that you are emptying him of his substance?

Why don't they stay where they belong?

Sure! That's easy enough to say: why don't they stay where they belong? The trouble is, they have been told they were French. They learned it in school. In the street. In the barracks. (Where they were given shoes to wear on their feet.) On the battlefields. They have had France squeezed into them wherever, in their bodies and in their souls, there was room for something apparently great.

Now they are told in no uncertain terms that they are in "our" country. That if they don't like it, all they have to do is go back to their Casbah. For here too there is a problem.

Whatever vicissitudes he may come up against in France, so some people claim, the North African will be happier at home . . .

It has been found in England that children who were magnificently fed, each having two nurses entirely at his service, but living away from the family circle, showed a morbidity twice as pronounced as children who were less well fed but who lived with their parents. Without going so far, think of all those who lead a life without a future in their own country and who refuse fine positions abroad. What is the good of a fine position if it does not culminate in a family, in something that can be called home?

Psychoanalytical science considers expatriation to be a morbid phenomenon. In which it is perfectly right.

These considerations allow us to conclude:

1. The North African will never be happier in Europe than at home, for he is asked to live without the very substance of his affectivity. Cut off from his origins and cut off from his ends, he is a thing tossed into the great sound and fury, bowed beneath the law of inertia.

2. There is something manifestly and abjectly disingenuous in the above statement. If the standard of living made available to the North African in France is higher than the one he was accustomed to at home, this means that there is still a good deal to be done in his country, in that "other part of France."

That there are houses to be built, schools to be opened, roads to be laid out, slums to be torn down, cities to be made to spring from the earth, men and women, children and children to be adorned with smiles.

This means that there is work to be done over there, human work, that is, work which is the meaning of a home. Not that of a room or a barrack building. It means that over the whole territory of the French nation (the metropolis and the French Union), there are tears to be wiped away, inhuman attitudes to be fought, condescending ways of speech to be ruled out, men to be humanized.

Your solution, sir?

Don't push me too far. Don't force me to tell you what you ought to know, sir. If YOU do not reclaim the man who is before you, how can I assume that you reclaim the man that is in you?

If YOU do not want the man who is before you, how can I believe the man that is perhaps in you?

If YOU do not demand the man, if YOU do not sacrifice the man that is in you so that the man who is on this earth shall be more than a body, more than a Mohammed, by what conjurer's trick will I have to acquire the certainty that you, too, are worthy of my love?

2

West Indians and Africans

Two years ago I was finishing a work[1] on the problem of the colored man in the white world. I knew that I must absolutely not amputate reality. I was not unaware of the fact that within the very entity of the "Negro people" movements could be discerned which, unfortunately, were utterly devoid of any attractive features. I mean, for example, that the enemy of the Negro is often not the white man but a man of his own color. This is why I suggested the possibility of a study which could contribute to the dissolution of the affective complexes that could oppose West Indians and Africans.

Before taking up the discussion we should like to point out that this business of Negroes is a dirty business. A business to turn your stomach. A business which, when you are faced with it, leaves you wholly disarmed if you accept the premises of the Negro-baiters. And when I say that the expression "Negro people" is an entity, I thereby indicate that, except for cultural influences, nothing is left. There is as great a difference between a West Indian and a Dakarian as between a Brazilian and a Spaniard. The object of lumping all Negroes together under the designation of "Negro people" is to deprive them of any possibility of individual expression. What is thus attempted is to put them under the obligation of matching the idea one has of them.

Is it not obvious that there can only be a white race? What would the "white people" correspond to? Do I have to explain the difference that exists between nation, people, fatherland,

First published in the review *Esprit*, February 1955.
[1] *Peau Noire et Masques Blancs* [Black Skin and White Masks]. Editions du Seuil, Paris.

community? When one says "Negro people," one systematically assumes that all Negroes agree on certain things, that they share a principle of communion. The truth is that there is nothing, *a priori*, to warrant the assumption that such a thing as a Negro people exists. That there is an African people, that there is a West Indian people, this I do believe.[2] But when someone talks to me about that "Negro people," I try to understand what is meant. Then, unfortunately, I understand that there is in this a source of conflicts. Then I try to destroy this source.

I shall be found to use terms like "metaphysical guilt," or "obsession with purity." I shall ask the reader not to be surprised: these will be accurate to the extent to which it is understood that since what is important cannot be attained, or more precisely, since what is important is not really sought after, one falls back on what is contingent. This is one of the laws of recrimination and of bad faith. The urgent thing is to rediscover what is important beneath what is contingent.

What is at issue here? I say that in a period of fifteen years a revolution has occurred in West Indian-African relations. I want to show wherein this event consists.

In Martinique it is rare to find hardened racial positions. The racial problem is covered over by economic discrimination and, in a given social class, it is above all productive of anecdotes. Relations are not modified by epidermal accentuations. Despite the greater or lesser amount of melanin that the skin may contain, there is a tacit agreement enabling all and sundry to recognize one another as doctors, tradesmen, workers. A Negro worker will be on the side of the mulatto worker against the middle-class Negro. Here we have proof that questions of race are but a superstructure, a mantle, an obscure ideological emanation concealing an economic reality.

In Martinique, when it is remarked that this or that person is in fact very black, this is said without contempt, without hatred.

---

[2] Let us say that the concessions we have made are fictitious. Philosophically and politically there is no such thing as an African people. There is an African world. And a West Indian world as well. On the other hand, it can be said that there is a Jewish people; but not a Jewish race.

One must be accustomed to what is called the spirit of Martinique in order to grasp the meaning of what is said. Jankelevitch has shown that irony is one of the forms that good conscience assumes. It is true that in the West Indies irony is a mechanism of defense against neurosis. A West Indian, in particular an intellectual who is no longer on the level of irony, discovers his Negritude. Thus, while in Europe irony protects against the existential anguish, in Martinique it protects against the awareness of Negritude.

It can be seen that a study of irony in the West Indies is crucial for the sociology of this region. Aggressiveness there is almost always cushioned by irony.[3]

It will be convenient for our purpose to distinguish two periods in the history of the West Indies: before and after the war of 1939-1945.

Before the War

Before 1939, the West Indian claimed to be happy, or at least thought of himself as being so.[4] He voted, went to school when he could, took part in the processions, liked rum and danced the beguine. Those who were privileged to go to France spoke of Paris, of Paris which meant France. And those who were not privileged to know Paris let themselves be beguiled.

There were also the civil servants working in Africa. Through them one saw a country of savages, of barbarians, of natives, of servants. Certain things need to be said if one is to avoid falsifying the problem. The metropolitan civil servant, returning from Africa, has accustomed us to stereotypes: sorcerers, makers of fetishes, tom-toms, guilelessness, faithfulness, respect for the white man, backwardness. The trouble is that the West Indian speaks of Africa in exactly the same way and, as the civil servant is not only the colonial administrator but the

---

[3] See, for example, the Carnival and the songs composed on this occasion.
[4] We might say: like the French lower middle class at this period, but that is not our point of approach. What we wish to do here is to study the change in attitude of the West Indian with respect to Negritude.

constable, the customs officer, the registrar, the soldier, at every
level of West Indian society an inescapable feeling of superiority over the African develops, becomes systematic, hardens. In
every West Indian, before the war of 1939, there was not only
the certainty of a superiority over the African, but the certainty
of a fundamental difference. The African was a Negro and the
West Indian a European.

These are things everyone gives the impression of knowing,
but which no one takes into account.

Before 1939 the West Indian who volunteered in the Colonial Army, whether he was illiterate or knew how to read and
write, served in a European unit, whereas the African, with the
exception of the natives of the five territories, served in a native
unit. The result to which we wish to draw attention is that,
whatever the field considered, the West Indian was superior to
the African, of a different species, assimilated to the metropolitan. But inasmuch as externally the West Indian was just a little
bit African, since, say what you will, he was black, he was
obliged—as a normal reaction in psychological economy—to
harden his frontiers in order to be protected against any mis-
apprehension.

We may say that the West Indian, not satisfied to be superior
to the African, despised him, and while the white man could
allow himself certain liberties with the native, the West Indian
absolutely could not. This was because, between whites and
Africans, there was no need of a reminder; the difference stared
one in the face. But what a catastrophe if the West Indian
should suddenly be taken for an African!

We may say also that this position of the West Indian was
authenticated by Europe. The West Indian was not a Negro; he
was a West Indian, that is to say a quasi-metropolitan. By this
attitude the white man justified the West Indian in his contempt for the African. The Negro, in short, was a man who
inhabited Africa.

In France, before 1940, when a West Indian was introduced
in Bordeaux or Paris society, the introducer always added,

"from Martinique." I say "Martinique," because—as people may or may not know—Guadeloupe, for some reason or other, was considered to be a country of savages. Even today, in 1952, we hear Martiniquans insist that they (the natives of Guadeloupe) are more savage than we are.

The African, for his part, was in Africa the real representative of the Negro race. As a matter of fact, when a boss made too great demands on a Martiniquan in a work situation, he would sometimes be told: "If it's a nigger you want, go and look for him in Africa," meaning thereby that slaves and forced labor had to be recruited elsewhere. Over there, where the Negroes were.

The African, on the other hand, apart from a few rare "developed" individuals, was looked down upon, despised, confined within the labyrinth of his epiderm. As we see, the positions were clear-cut: on the one hand, the African; on the other, the European and the West Indian. The West Indian was a black man, but the Negro was in Africa.

In 1939 no West Indian in the West Indies proclaimed himself to be a Negro, claimed to be a Negro. When he did, it was always in his relations with a white man. It was the white man, the "bad white man," who obliged him to assert his color, more exactly to defend it. But it can be affirmed that in the West Indies in 1939 no spontaneous claim of Negritude rang forth.

It was then that three events occurred successively.

The first event was the arrival of Césaire.

For the first time a *lycée* teacher—a man, therefore, who was apparently worthy of respect—was seen to announce quite simply to West Indian society "that it is fine and good to be a Negro." To be sure, this created a scandal. It was said at the time that he was a little mad and his colleagues went out of their way to give details as to his supposed ailment.

What indeed could be more grotesque than an educated man, a man with a diploma, having in consequence understood a good many things, among others that "it was unfortunate to be a Negro," proclaiming that his skin was beautiful and that the *"big black hole"* was a source of truth. Neither the mulattoes nor the Negroes understood this delirium. The mulattoes because they had escaped from the night, the Negroes because they aspired to get away from it. Two centuries of white truth proved this man to be wrong. He must be mad, for it was unthinkable that he could be right.

Once the excitement had died down, everything seemed to resume its normal course . . . And Césaire was about to be proved wrong, when the second event occurred: I am referring to the French defeat.

The downfall of France, for the West Indian, was in a sense the murder of the father. This national defeat might have been endured as it was in the metropolis, but a good part of the French fleet remained blockaded in the West Indies during the four years of the German occupation. This needs to be emphasized. I believe it is essential to grasp the historic importance of those four years.

Before 1939 there were about two thousand Europeans in Martinique. These Europeans had well-defined functions, were integrated into the social life, involved in the country's economy. Now from one day to the next, the single town of Fort-de-France was submerged by nearly ten thousand Europeans having an unquestionable, but until then latent, racist mentality. I mean that the sailors of the *Béarn* or the *Emile-Bertin,* on previous occasions in the course of a week in Fort-de-France, had not had time to manifest their racial prejudices. The four years during which they were obliged to live shut in on themselves, inactive, a prey to anguish when they thought of their families left in France, victims of despair as to the future, allowed them to drop a mask which, when all is said and done, was rather superficial, and to behave as "authentic racists."

It may be added that the West Indian economy suffered a severe blow, for it became necessary to find—again without any transition—at a time when nothing could be imported, the wherewithal to feed ten thousand men. Moreover, many of those sailors and soldiers were able to send for their wives and children, who had to be housed. The Martiniquan held those white racists responsible for all this. The West Indian, in the presence of those men who despised him, began to have misgivings as to his values. The West Indian underwent his first metaphysical experience.

Then came Free France. De Gaulle, in London, spoke of treason, of soldiers who surrendered their swords even before they had drawn them. All this contributed to convincing the West Indians that France, *their* France, had not lost the war but that traitors had sold it out. And where were these traitors, if not camouflaged in the West Indies? One then witnessed an extraordinary sight: West Indians refusing to take off their hats while the *Marseillaise* was being played. What West Indian can forget those Thursday evenings when on the Esplanade de la Savane, patrols of armed sailors demanded silence and attention while the national anthem was being played? What had happened?

By a process easy to understand, the West Indians had assimilated the France of the sailors into the bad France, and the *Marseillaise* that those men respected was not their own. It must not be forgotten that those sailors were racists. Now "everybody knows that the true Frenchman is not a racist; in other words, he does not consider the West Indian a Negro." Since these men did so consider him, this meant that they were not true Frenchmen. Who knows, perhaps they were Germans? And as a matter of fact, the sailor was systematically considered as a German. But the consequence that concerns us is the following: before ten thousand racists, the West Indian felt obliged to defend himself. Without Césaire this would have been difficult for him. But Césaire was there, and people joined him in chanting the once-hated song to the effect that it is fine and good to be a Negro! . . .

For two years the West Indian defended his "virtuous color" inch by inch and, without suspecting it, was dancing on the edge of a precipice. For after all, if the color black is virtuous, I shall be all the more virtuous the blacker I am! Then there emerged from the shadows the very black, the "blues," the pure. And Césaire, the faithful bard, would repeat that "paint the tree trunk white as you will, the roots below remain black." Then it became real that not only the color black was invested with value, but fiction black, ideal black, black in the absolute, primitive black, the Negro. This amounted to nothing less than requiring the West Indian totally to recast his world, to undergo a metamorphosis of his body. It meant demanding of him an axiological activity in reverse, a valorization of what he had rejected.

But history continued. In 1943, weary of an ostracism to which they were not accustomed, irritated, famished, the West Indians, who had formerly been separated into closed sociological groups, broke all barriers, came to an agreement on certain things, among others that those Germans had gone too far and, supported by the local army, fought for and won the rallying of the colony to the Free French. Admiral Robert, "that other German," yielded. And this leads us to the third event.

It can be said that the demonstrations on the occasion of the Liberation, which were held in the West Indies, in any case in Martinique, in the months of July and August 1943, were the consequence of the birth of the proletariat. Martinique for the first time systematized its political consciousness. It is logical that the elections that followed the Liberation should have delegated two communist deputies out of three. In Martinique, the first metaphysical, or if one prefers, ontological experiment, coincided with the first political experiment. Auguste Comte regarded the proletarian as a systematic philosopher. The proletarian of Martinique is a systematized Negro.

After the War

Thus the West Indian, after 1945, changed his values. Whereas before 1939 he had his eyes riveted on white Europe, whereas what seemed good to him was escape from his color, in 1945 he discovered himself to be not only black but a Negro, and it was in the direction of distant Africa that he was henceforth to put out his feelers. The West Indian in France was continually recalling that he was not a Negro: from 1945 on, the West Indian in France was continually to recall that he *was* a Negro.

During this time the African pursued his way. He was not torn; he did not have to situate himself simultaneously with reference to the West Indian and with reference to the European. These last belonged in the same bag, the bag of the starvers, of the exploiters, of the no-goods. To be sure, there had been Eboué, who though a West Indian, had spoken to the Africans at the Brazzaville conference and had called them "my dear brothers." And this brotherhood was not evangelical; it was based on color. The Africans had adopted Eboué. He was one of them. The other West Indians could come, but their pretensions to superiority were known. But to the Africans' great astonishment, the West Indians who came to Africa after 1945 appeared with their hands stretched out, their backs bowed, humbly suppliant. They came to Africa with their hearts full of hope, eager to rediscover the source, to suckle at the authentic breasts of the African earth. The West Indians, civil servants and military, lawyers and doctors, landing in Dakar, were distressed at not being sufficiently black. Fifteen years before, they said to the Europeans, "Don't pay attention to my black skin, it's the sun that has burned me, my soul is as white as yours." After 1945 they changed their tune. They said to the Africans, "Don't pay attention to my white skin, my soul is as black as yours, and that is what matters."

But the Africans were too resentful of them to allow them so easy a turnabout. Recognized in their blackness, in their obscurity, in what fifteen years before had been sin, they resented any encroachment on the West Indian's part in this realm. They discovered themselves at last to be the possessors of truth, centuries-old bearers of an incorruptible purity. They rejected the West Indian, reminding him that *they* had not deserted, that *they* had not betrayed, that *they* had toiled, suffered, struggled on the African earth. The West Indian had said no to the white man; the African was saying no to the West Indian.

The latter was undergoing his second metaphysical experience. He then suffered despair. Haunted by impurity, overwhelmed by sin, riddled with guilt, he was prey to the tragedy of being neither white nor Negro.

He wept, he composed poems, sang of Africa, of Africa the hard and the beautiful, Africa exploding with anger, tumultuous bustle, splash, Africa land of truth. At the Institute of Oriental Languages in Paris he learned Bambara. The African, in his majesty, rejected all approaches. The African was getting his revenge and the West Indian was paying . . .

If we now try to explain and summarize the situation, we may say that in Martinque, before 1939, there was not on one side the Negro and on the other side the white man, but a scale of colors the intervals of which could readily be passed over. One needed only to have children by someone less black than oneself. There was no racial barrier, no discrimination. There was that ironic spice, so characteristic of the Martinique mentality.

But in Africa the discrimination was real. There the Negro, the African, the native, the black, the dirty, was rejected, despised, cursed. There an amputation had occurred; there humanity was denied.

Until 1939 the West Indian lived, thought, dreamed (we have shown this in *Black Skin, White Masks*), composed poems, wrote novels exactly as a white man would have done. We understand now why it was not possible for him, as for the African poets, to sing the black night, "The black woman with pink heels." Before Césaire, West Indian literature was a literature of Europeans. The West Indian identified himself with the white man, adopted a white man's attitude, "was a white man."

After the West Indian was obliged, under the pressure of European racists, to abandon positions which were essentially fragile, because they were absurd, because they were incorrect, because they were alienating, a new generation came into being. The West Indian of 1945 is a Negro.

In *Cahier d'un retour au pays natal* (logbook of a return to the native land) there is an African period, for on page 49 we read:

> *By dint of thinking of the Congo*
> *I have become a Congo humming with forests and rivers*

Then, with his eyes on Africa, the West Indian was to hail it. He discovered himself to be a transplanted son of slaves; he felt the vibration of Africa in the very depth of his body and aspired only to one thing: to plunge into the great "black hole."

It thus seems that the West Indian, after the great white error, is now living in the great black mirage.

II

Racism and Culture

The unilaterally decreed normative value of certain cultures deserves our careful attention. One of the paradoxes immediately encountered is the rebound of egocentric, sociocentric definitions.

There is first affirmed the existence of human groups having no culture; then of a hierarchy of cultures; and finally, the concept of cultural relativity.

We have here the whole range from overall negation to singular and specific recognition. It is precisely this fragmented and bloody history that we must sketch on the level of cultural anthropology.

There are, we may say, certain constellations of institutions, established by particular men, in the framework of precise geographical areas, which at a given moment have undergone a direct and sudden assault of different cultural patterns. The technical, generally advanced development of the social group that has thus appeared enables it to set up an organized domination. The enterprise of deculturation turns out to be the negative of a more gigantic work of economic, and even biological, enslavement.

The doctrine of cultural hierarchy is thus but one aspect of a systematized hierarchization implacably pursued.

The modern theory of the absence of cortical integration of colonial peoples is the anatomic-physiological counterpart of this doctrine. The apparition of racism is not fundamentally

Text of Frantz Fanon's speech before the First Congress of Negro Writers and Artists in Paris, September 1956. Published in the Special Issue of *Présence Africaine*, June-November, 1956.

determining. Racism is not the whole but the most visible, the most day-to-day and, not to mince matters, the crudest element of a given structure.

To study the relations of racism and culture is to raise the question of their reciprocal action. If culture is the combination of motor and mental behavior patterns arising from the encounter of man with nature and with his fellow-man, it can be said that racism is indeed a cultural element. There are thus cultures with racism and cultures without racism.

This precise cultural element, however, has not become encysted. Racism has not managed to harden. It has had to renew itself, to adapt itself, to change its appearance. It has had to undergo the fate of the cultural whole that informed it.

The vulgar, primitive, over-simple racism purported to find in biology—the Scriptures having proved insufficient—the material basis of the doctrine. It would be tedious to recall the efforts then undertaken: the comparative form of the skulls, the quantity and the configuration of the folds of the brain, the characteristics of the cell layers of the cortex, the dimensions of the vertebrae, the microscopic appearance of the epiderm, etc. . . .

Intellectual and emotional primitivism appeared as a banal consequence, a recognition of existence.

Such affirmations, crude and massive, give way to a more refined argument. Here and there, however, an occasional relapse is to be noted. Thus the "emotional instability of the Negro," the "subcritical integration of the Arab," the "quasi-generic culpability of the Jew" are data that one comes upon among a few contemporary writers. The monograph by J. Carothers, for example, sponsored by the World Health Organization, invokes "scientific arguments" in support of a physiological lobotomy of the African Negro.

These old-fashioned positions tend in any case to disappear. This racism that aspires to be rational, individual, genotypically and phenotypically determined, becomes transformed into cultural racism. The object of racism is no longer the individual man but a certain form of existing. At the extreme, such terms as "message" and "cultural style" are resorted to. "Occidental values" oddly blend with the already famous appeal to the fight of the "cross against the crescent."

The morphological equation, to be sure, has not totally disappeared, but events of the past thirty years have shaken the most solidly anchored convictions, upset the checkerboard, restructured a great number of relationships.

The memory of Nazism, the common wretchedness of different men, the common enslavement of extensive social groups, the apparition of "European colonies," in other words the institution of a colonial system in the very heart of Europe, the growing awareness of workers in the colonizing and racist countries, the evolution of techniques, all this has deeply modified the problem and the manner of approaching it.

We must look for the consequences of this racism on the cultural level.

Racism, as we have seen, is only one element of a vaster whole: that of the systematized oppression of a people. How does an oppressing people behave? Here we rediscover constants.

We witness the destruction of cultural values, of ways of life. Language, dress, techniques, are devalorized. How can one account for this constant? Psychologists, who tend to explain everything by movements of the psyche, claim to discover this behavior on the level of contacts between individuals: the criticism of an original hat, of a way of speaking, of walking . . .

Such attempts deliberately leave out of account the special character of the colonial situation. In reality the nations that undertake a colonial war have no concern for the confrontation of cultures. War is a gigantic business and every approach must be governed by this datum. The enslavement, in the strictest sense, of the native population is the prime necessity.

For this its systems of reference have to be broken. Expropriation, spoliation, raids, objective murder, are matched by the sacking of cultural patterns, or at least condition such sacking. The social panorama is destructured; values are flaunted, crushed, emptied.

The lines of force, having crumbled, no longer give direction.

In their stead a new system of values is imposed, not proposed but affirmed, by the heavy weight of cannons and sabers.

The setting up of the colonial system does not of itself bring about the death of the native culture. Historic observation reveals, on the contrary, that the aim sought is rather a continued agony than a total disappearance of the pre-existing culture. This culture, once living and open to the future, becomes closed, fixed in the colonial status, caught in the yoke of oppression. Both present and mummified, it testifies against its members. It defines them in fact without appeal. The cultural mummification leads to a mummification of individual thinking. The apathy so universally noted among colonial peoples is but the logical consequence of this operation. The reproach of inertia constantly directed at "the native" is utterly dishonest. As though it were possible for a man to evolve otherwise than within the framework of a culture that recognizes him and that he decides to assume.

Thus we witness the setting up of archaic, inert institutions, functioning under the oppressor's supervision and patterned like a caricature of formerly fertile institutions . . .

These bodies appear to embody respect for the tradition, the cultural specificities, the personality of the subjugated people. This pseudo-respect in fact is tantamount to the most utter contempt, to the most elaborate sadism. The characteristic of a culture is to be open, permeated by spontaneous, generous, fertile lines of force. The appointment of "reliable men" to execute certain gestures is a deception that deceives no one. Thus the Kabyle *djemaas* named by the French authority are not recognized by the natives. They are matched by another *djemaa* democratically elected. And naturally the second as a rule dictates to the first what his conduct should be.

The constantly affirmed concern with "respecting the culture of the native populations" accordingly does not signify taking into consideration the values borne by the culture, incarnated by men. Rather, this behavior betrays a determination to objectify, to confine, to imprison, to harden. Phrases such as "I know them," "that's the way they are," show this maximum objectification successfully achieved. I can think of gestures and thoughts that define these men.

Exoticism is one of the forms of this simplification. It allows no cultural confrontation. There is on the one hand a culture in which qualities of dynamism, of growth, of depth can be recognized. As against this, we find characteristics, curiosities, things, never a structure.

Thus in an initial phase the occupant establishes his domination, massively affirms his superiority. The social group, militarily and economically subjugated, is dehumanized in accordance with a polydimensional method.

Exploitation, tortures, raids, racism, collective liquidations, rational oppression take turns at different levels in order literally to make of the native an object in the hands of the occupying nation.

This object man, without means of existing, without a *raison d'être*, is broken in the very depth of his substance. The desire to live, to continue, becomes more and more indecisive, more and more phantom-like. It is at this stage that the well-known guilt complex appears. In his first novels, Wright gives a very detailed description of it.

Progressively, however, the evolution of techniques of production, the industrialization, limited though it is, of the subjugated countries, the increasingly necessary existence of collaborators, impose a new attitude upon the occupant. The complexity of the means of production, the evolution of economic relations inevitably involving the evolution of ideologies, unbalance the system. Vulgar racism in its biological form corresponds to the period of crude exploitation of man's arms and legs. The perfecting of the means of production inevitably brings about the camouflage of the techniques by which man is exploited, hence of the forms of racism.

It is therefore not as a result of the evolution of people's minds that racism loses its virulence. No inner revolution can explain this necessity for racism to seek more subtle forms, to evolve. On all sides men become free, putting an end to the lethargy to which oppression and racism had condemned them.

In the very heart of the "civilized nations" the workers finally discover that the exploitation of man, at the root of a system, assumes different faces. At this stage racism no longer dares appear without disguise. It is unsure of itself. In an ever greater number of circumstances the racist takes to cover. He who claimed to "sense," to "see through" those others, finds himself to be a target, looked at, judged. The racist's purpose has become a purpose haunted by bad conscience. He can find salvation only in a passion-driven commitment such as is found in certain psychoses. And having defined the symptomatology of such passion-charged deliria is not the least of Professor Baruk's merits.

Racism is never a super-added element discovered by chance in the course of the investigation of the cultural data of a group. The social constellation, the cultural whole, are deeply modified by the existence of racism.

It is a common saying nowadays that racism is a plague of humanity. But we must not content ourselves with such a phrase. We must tirelessly look for the repercussions of racism at all levels of sociability. The importance of the racist problem in contemporary American literature is significant. The Negro in motion pictures, the Negro and folklore, the Jew and children's stories, the Jew in the café, are inexhaustible themes.

Racism, to come back to America, haunts and vitiates American culture. And this dialectical gangrene is exacerbated by the coming to awareness and the determination of millions of Negroes and Jews to fight this racism by which they are victimized.

This passion-charged, irrational, groundless phase, when one examines it, reveals a frightful visage. The movement of groups, the liberation, in certain parts of the world, of men previously kept down, make for a more and more precarious equilibrium. Rather unexpectedly, the racist group points accusingly to a manifestation of racism among the oppressed. The "intellectual primitivism" of the period of exploitation gives way to the "medieval, in fact prehistoric fanaticism" of the period of the liberation.

For a time it looked as though racism had disappeared. This soul-soothing, unreal impression was simply the consequence of the evolution of forms of exploitation. Psychologists spoke of a prejudice having become unconscious. The truth is that the rigor of the system made the daily affirmation of a superiority superfluous. The need to appeal to various degrees of approval and support, to the native's cooperation, modified relations in a less crude, more subtle, more "cultivated" direction. It was not rare, in fact, to see a "democratic and humane" ideology at this stage. The commercial undertaking of enslavement, of cultural destruction, progressively gave way to a verbal mystification.

The interesting thing about this evolution is that racism was taken as a topic of meditation, sometimes even as a publicity technique.

Thus the blues—"the black slave lament"—was offered up for the admiration of the oppressors. This modicum of stylized oppression is the exploiter's and the racist's rightful due. Without oppression and without racism you have no blues. The end of racism would sound the knell of great Negro music . . .

As the all-too-famous Toynbee might say, the blues are the slave's response to the challenge of oppression.

Still today, for many men, even colored, Armstrong's music has a real meaning only in this perspective.

Racism bloats and disfigures the face of the culture that practices it. Literature, the plastic arts, songs for shopgirls, proverbs, habits, patterns, whether they set out to attack it or to vulgarize it, restore racism. This means that a social group, a country, a civilization, cannot be unconsciously racist.

We say once again that racism is not an accidental discovery. It is not a hidden, dissimulated element. No superhuman efforts are needed to bring it out.

Racism stares one in the face for it so happens that it belongs in a characteristic whole: that of the shameless exploitation of one group of men by another which has reached a higher stage of technical development. This is why military and economic oppression generally precedes, makes possible, and legitimizes racism.

The habit of considering racism as a mental quirk, as a psychological flaw, must be abandoned.

But the men who are a prey to racism, the enslaved, exploited, weakened social group—how do they behave? What are their defense mechanisms?

What attitudes do we discover here?

In an initial phase we have seen the occupying power legitimizing its domination by scientific arguments, the "inferior race" being denied on the basis of race. Because no other solution is left it, the racialized social group tries to imitate the oppressor and thereby to deracialize itself. The "inferior race" denies itself as a different race. It shares with the "superior race" the convictions, doctrines, and other attitudes concerning it.

Having witnessed the liquidation of its systems of reference, the collapse of its cultural patterns, the native can only recognize with the occupant that "God is not on his side." The oppressor, through the inclusive and frightening character of his authority, manages to impose on the native new ways of seeing, and in particular a pejorative judgment with respect to his original forms of existing.

This event, which is commonly designated as alienation, is naturally very important. It is found in the official texts under the name of assimilation.

Now this alienation is never wholly successful. Whether or not it is because the oppressor quantitatively and qualitatively limits the evolution, unforeseen, disparate phenomena manifest themselves.

The inferiorized group had admitted, since the force of reasoning was implacable, that its misfortunes resulted directly from its racial and cultural characteristics.

Guilt and inferiority are the usual consequences of this dialectic. The oppressed then tries to escape these, on the one hand by proclaiming his total and unconditional adoption of the new cultural models, and on the other, by pronouncing an irreversible condemnation of his own cultural style.[1]

Yet the necessity that the oppressor encounters at a given point to dissimulate the forms of exploitation does not lead to the disappearance of this exploitation. The more elaborate, less crude economic relations require a daily coating, but the alienation at this level remains frightful.

Having judged, condemned, abandoned his cultural forms, his language, his food habits, his sexual behavior, his way of sitting down, of resting, of laughing, of enjoying himself, the oppressed *flings himself* upon the imposed culture with the desperation of a drowning man.

Developing his technical knowledge in contact with more and more perfected machines, entering into the dynamic circuit of industrial production, meeting men from remote regions in the framework of the concentration of capital, that is to say, on the job, discovering the assembly line, the team, production "time," in other words yield per hour, the oppressed is shocked to find that he continues to be the object of racism and contempt.

It is at this level that racism is treated as a question of persons. "There are a few hopeless racists, but you must admit that on the whole the population likes . . ."

With time all this will disappear.

This is the country where there is the least amount of race prejudice . . .

At the United Nations there is a commission to fight race prejudice.

Films on race prejudice, poems on race prejudice, messages on race prejudice . . .

Spectacular and futile condemnations of race prejudice. In

---

[1] A little-studied phenomenon sometimes appears at this stage. Intellectuals, students, belonging to the dominant group, make "scientific" studies of the dominated society, its art, its ethical universe.

In the universities the rare colonized intellectuals find their own cultural system being revealed to them. It even happens that scholars of the colonizing countries grow enthusiastic over this or that specific feature. The concepts of purity, naïveté, innocence appear. The native intellectual's vigilance must here be doubly on the alert.

reality, a colonial country is a racist country. If in England, in Belgium, or in France, despite the democratic principles affirmed by these respective nations, there are still racists, it is these racists who, in their opposition to the country as a whole, are logically consistent.

It is not possible to enslave men without logically making them inferior through and through. And racism is only the emotional, affective, sometimes intellectual explanation of this inferiorization.

The racist in a culture with racism is therefore normal. He has achieved a perfect harmony of economic relations and ideology. The idea that one forms of man, to be sure, is never totally dependent on economic relations, in other words—and this must not be forgotten—on relations existing historically and geographically among men and groups. An ever greater number of members belonging to racist societies are taking a position. They are dedicating themselves to a world in which racism would be impossible. But everyone is not up to this kind of objectivity, this abstraction, this solemn commitment. One cannot with impunity require of a man that he be against "the prejudices of his group."

And, we repeat, every colonialist group is racist.

"Acculturized" and deculturized at one and the same time, the oppressed continues to come up against racism. He finds this sequel illogical, what he has left behind him inexplicable, without motive, incorrect. His knowledge, the appropriation of precise and complicated techniques, sometimes his intellectual superiority as compared to a great number of racists, lead him to qualify the racist world as passion-charged. He perceives that the racist atmosphere impregnates all the elements of the social life. The sense of an overwhelming injustice is correspondingly very strong. Forgetting racism as a consequence, one concentrates on racism as cause. Campaigns of deintoxication are launched. Appeal is made to the sense of humanity, to love, to respect for the supreme values . . .

Race prejudice in fact obeys a flawless logic. A country that lives, draws its substance from the exploitation of other peoples, makes those peoples inferior. Race prejudice applied to those peoples is normal.

Racism is therefore not a constant of the human spirit.

It is, as we have seen, a disposition fitting into a well-defined system. And anti-Jewish prejudice is no different from anti-Negro prejudice. A society has race prejudice or it has not. There are no degrees of prejudice. One cannot say that a given country is racist but that lynchings or extermination camps are not to be found there. The truth is that all that and still other things exist on the horizon. These virtualities, these latencies circulate, carried by the life-stream of psycho-affective, economic relations . . .

Discovering the futility of his alienation, his progressive deprivation, the inferiorized individual, after this phase of deculturation, of extraneousness, comes back to his original positions.

This culture, abandoned, sloughed off, rejected, despised, becomes for the inferiorized an object of passionate attachment. There is a very marked kind of overvaluation that is psychologically closely linked to the craving for forgiveness.

But behind this simplifying analysis there is indeed the intuition experienced by the inferiorized of having discovered a spontaneous truth. This is a psychological datum that is part of the texture of History and of Truth.

Because the inferiorized rediscovers a style that had once been devalorized, what he does is in fact to cultivate culture. Such a caricature of cultural existence would indicate, if it were necessary, that culture must be lived, and cannot be fragmented. It cannot be had piecemeal.

Yet the oppressed goes into ecstasies over each rediscovery. The wonder is permanent. Having formerly emigrated from his culture, the native today explores it with ardor. It is a continual honeymoon. Formerly inferiorized, he is now in a state of grace.

Not with impunity, however, does one undergo domination. The culture of the enslaved people is sclerosed, dying. No life any longer circulates in it. Or more precisely, the only existing life is dissimulated. The population that normally assumes here and there a few fragments of life, which continues to attach dynamic meanings to institutions, is an anonymous population. In a colonial system these are the traditionalists.

The former emigré, by the sudden ambiguity of his behavior, causes consternation. To the anonymity of the traditionalist he opposes a vehement and aggressive exhibitionism.

The state of grace and aggressiveness are the two constants found at this stage. Aggressiveness being the passion-charged mechanism making it possible to escape the sting of paradox.

Because the former emigré is in possession of precise techniques, because his level of action is in the framework of relations that are already complex, these rediscoveries assume an irrational aspect. There is an hiatus, a discrepancy between intellectual development, technical appropriation, highly differentiated modes of thinking and of logic, on the one hand, and a "simple, pure" emotional basis on the other . . .

Rediscovering tradition, living it as a defense mechanism, as a symbol of purity, of salvation, the decultured individual leaves the impression that the mediation takes vengeance by substantializing itself. This falling back on archaic positions having no relation to technical development is paradoxical. The institutions thus valorized no longer correspond to the elaborate methods of action already mastered.

The culture put into capsules, which has vegetated since the foreign domination, is revalorized. It is not reconceived, grasped anew, dynamized from within. It is shouted. And this headlong, unstructured, verbal revalorization conceals paradoxical attitudes.

It is at this point that the incorrigible character of the inferiorized is brought out for mention. Arab doctors sleep on the ground, spit all over the place, etc. . . .

Negro intellectuals consult a sorcerer before making a decision, etc. . . .

"Collaborating" intellectuals try to justify their new attitude.

The customs, traditions, beliefs, formerly denied and passed over in silence are violently valorized and affirmed.

Tradition is no longer scoffed at by the group. The group no longer runs away from itself. The sense of the past is rediscovered, the worship of ancestors resumed . . .

The past, becoming henceforth a constellation of values, becomes identified with the Truth.

This rediscovery, this absolute valorization almost in defiance of reality, objectively indefensible, assumes an incomparable and subjective importance. On emerging from these passionate espousals, the native will have decided, "with full knowledge of what is involved," to fight all forms of exploitation and of alienation of man. At this same time, the occupant, on the other hand, multiplies appeals to assimilation, then to integration, to community.

The native's hand-to-hand struggle with his culture is too solemn, too abrupt an operation to tolerate the slighest slip-up. No neologism can mask the new certainty: the plunge into the chasm of the past is the condition and the source of freedom.

The logical end of this will to struggle is the total liberation of the national territory. In order to achieve this liberation, the inferiorized man brings all his resources into play, all his acquisitions, the old and the new, his own and those of the occupant.

The struggle is at once total, absolute. But then race prejudice is hardly found to appear.

At the time of imposing his domination, in order to justify slavery, the oppressor had invoked scientific argument. There is nothing of the kind here.

A people that undertakes a struggle for liberation rarely legitimizes race prejudice. Even in the course of acute periods of insurrectional armed struggle one never witnesses the recourse to biological justifications.

The struggle of the inferiorized is situated on a markedly more human level. The perspectives are radically new. The opposition is the henceforth classical one of the struggles of conquest and of liberation.

In the course of struggle the dominating nation tries to revive racist arguments but the elaboration of racism proves more and more ineffective. There is talk of fanaticism, of primitive attitudes in the face of death, but once again the now crumbling mechanism no longer responds. Those who were once unbudgeable, the constitutional cowards, the timid, the eternally inferiorized, stiffen and emerge bristling.

The occupant is bewildered.

The end of race prejudice begins with a sudden incomprehension.

The occupant's spasmed and rigid culture, now liberated, opens at last to the culture of people who have really become brothers. The two cultures can affront each other, enrich each other.

In conclusion, universality resides in this decision to recognize and accept the reciprocal relativism of different cultures, once the colonial status is irreversibly excluded.

III

For Algeria

1

Letter to a Frenchman

When you told me you wanted to leave Algeria, my friendship suddenly assumed the cloak of silence. Images, stubborn and sharp, sprang forth in the gateway of my memory.

I was looking at you and at your wife beside you.

I saw you already in France . . . New faces around you, very far from the country where for some time now things are certainly not going well.

You told me the atmosphere is getting rotten, I must leave. Your decision, without being irrevocable because you had expressed it, was progressively taking shape.

How inexplicably the country bristles! The roads no longer safe. The wheat fields transformed into sheets of flame. The Arabs becoming hostile.

People talk. People talk.

The women will be raped. Men will have their testicles cut off and rammed between their teeth.

Remember Sétif! Do you want to see another Sétif?[1]

They will, but we won't.

All this you told me, laughing.

But your wife wasn't laughing.

And behind your laugh I saw.

I saw your essential ignorance of this country and its ways.

I'll tell you what I mean.

Perhaps you will leave, but tell me, when you are asked, "What is going on in Algeria?" what will you answer?

[1] Sétif was a central point in the Moslem uprising that occurred in the region of Kabylia in May 1945. In the repression which followed, lasting some two weeks, aviation and artillery took a heavy toll of lives.—*Tr.*

When your brothers ask you: "What has happened in Algeria?" what will you answer them?

More precisely, when people will want to know why you left this country, what will you do to stifle the shame that already burdens you?

The shame of not having understood, of not having wanted to understand what has happened around you every day.

For eight years you have been in this country.

And no part of this enormous wound has held you back in any way.

And no part of this enormous wound has pushed you in any way.

You have been free to discover yourself at last such as you are.

Concerned about Man but strangely not about the Arab.

Worried, anguished, torn.

But right out in the open, your immersion in the same mud, in the same leprosy.

For there is not a European who is not revolted, indignant, alarmed at everything, except at the fate to which the Arab is subjected.

Unperceived Arabs.

Ignored Arabs.

Arabs passed over in silence.

Arabs spirited away, dissimulated.

Arabs daily denied, transformed into the Saharan stage set. And you mingling with those:

Who have never shaken hands with an Arab.

Never drunk coffee.

Never exchanged commonplaces about the weather with an Arab.

By your side the Arabs.

Pushed aside the Arabs.

Without effort rejected the Arabs.

Confined the Arabs.

Native town crushed.

Town of sleeping natives.

Nothing ever happens among the Arabs.

All this leprosy on your body.

You will leave. But all these questions, these questions without answer. The collective silence of 800,000 Frenchmen, this ignorant silence, this innocent silence.

And 9,000,000 men under this winding-sheet of silence.

I offer you this dossier so that no one will die, neither yesterday's dead, nor the resuscitated of today.

I want my voice to be harsh, I don't want it to be beautiful, I don't want it to be pure, I don't want it to have all dimensions.

I want it to be torn through and through, I don't want it to be enticing, for I am speaking of man and his refusal, of the day-to-day rottenness of man, of his dreadful failure.

I want you to tell.

That I should say for example: there is a shortage of schools in Algeria, so that you will think: it's a shame, something has to be done about it.

That I should say: one Arab out of three hundred is able to sign his name, so that you will think: that's too bad, it has to stop.

Listen further:

A school-mistress complaining to me, complaining about having to admit new Arab children to her school every year.

A school mistress complaining that once all the Europeans were enrolled, she was obliged to give schooling to a few Arab children.

The illiteracy of these "Ayrab" tots that spreads at the same rate as our silence.

Teach the Arabs? You're not serious.

So you just want to complicate our lives.

They're fine the way they are.

The less they understand the better off they are.

And where would we get the funds?

It will cost you a fortune.

Anyway, they're not asking for that much.

A survey carried out among the *Caïds* shows that the Arab doesn't demand schools.[2]

Millions of young bootblacks. Millions of *"porter, madame?"*

Millions of give me a piece of bread. Millions of illiterates "not knowing how to sign, don't sign, let us sign."

Millions of fingerprints on the police reports that lead to prisons.

On Monsieur le Cadi's records.

On the enlistments in the regiments of Algerian infantry.

Millions of *fellahs* exploited, cheated, robbed.[3]

Fellahs grabbed at four in the morning,

Released at eight in the evening.

From sun to moon.

Fellahs gorged with water, gorged with leaves, gorged with old biscuit which has to last all month.

Motionless *fellah* and your arms move and your bowed back but your life stopped. The cars pass and you don't move. They could run over your belly and you wouldn't move.

Arabs on the roads.

Sticks slipped through the handle of the basket.

Empty basket, empty hope, this whole death of the *fellah*.

Two hundred fifty francs a day.

Fellah without land.

Fellah without reason.

If you don't like it you can just leave. Shacks full of children. Shacks full of women.

Wrung-out *fellah*.

Without dream.

Six times two hundred fifty francs a day.

And nothing here belongs to you.

We're nice to you, what are you complaining about?

What would you do without us? A fine country this would be if we left!

Become a swamp in no time at all, yes!

---

[2] A *caïd* is an indigenous magistrate.—*Tr.*
[3] A *fellah* is a peasant.—*Tr.*

Twenty-four times two hundred fifty francs a day.

Work *fellah*. In your blood the prostrate exhaustion of a whole lifetime.

Six thousand francs a month.

On your face despair.

In your belly resignation . . .

What does it matter *fellah* if this country is beautiful.

2

Letter to the Resident Minister (1956)

Monsieur le Docteur Frantz Fanon
Médecin des Hôpitaux Psychiatriques
Médecin-Chef de Service à
l'Hôpital Psychiatrique de
BLIDA-JOINVILLE

à Monsieur le Ministre Résident,
Gouverneur Général de l'Algérie
ALGER

Monsieur le Ministre,

At my request and by decree under date of October 22, 1953, the Minister of Public Health and Population was good enough to put me at the disposal of the Governor-General of Algeria to be assigned to a Psychiatric Hospital in Algeria.

Having been given a post at the Psychiatric Hospital of Blida-Joinville on November 23, 1953, I have since that date performed the duties of medical director here.

Although the objective conditions under which psychiatry is practiced in Algeria constituted a challenge to common sense, it appeared to me that an effort should be made to attenuate the viciousness of a system of which the doctrinal foundations are a daily defiance of an authentically human outlook.

For nearly three years I have placed myself wholly at the service of this country and of the men who inhabit it. I have spared neither my efforts nor my enthusiasm. There is not a parcel of my activity that has not had as its objective the unanimously hoped-for emergence of a better world.

But what can a man's enthusiasm and devotion achieve if everyday reality is a tissue of lies, of cowardice, of contempt for man?

What good are intentions if their realization is made impossible by the indigence of the heart, the sterility of the mind, the hatred of the natives of this country?

Madness is one of the means man has of losing his freedom. And I can say, on the basis of what I have been able to observe from this point of vantage, that the degree of alienation of the inhabitants of this country appears to me frightening.

If psychiatry is the medical technique that aims to enable man no longer to be a stranger to his environment, I owe it to myself to affirm that the Arab, permanently an alien in his own country, lives in a state of absolute depersonalization.

What is the status of Algeria? A systematized de-humanization.

It was an absurd gamble to undertake, at whatever cost, to bring into existence a certain number of values, when the lawlessness, the inequality, the multi-daily murder of man were raised to the status of legislative principles.

The social structure existing in Algeria was hostile to any attempt to put the individual back where he belonged.

Monsieur le Ministre, there comes a moment when tenacity becomes morbid perseverance. Hope is then no longer an open door to the future but the illogical maintenance of a subjective attitude in organized contradiction with reality.

Monsieur le Ministre, the present-day events that are steeping Algeria in blood do not constitute a scandal for the observer. What is happening is the result neither of an accident nor of a breakdown in the mechanism.

The events in Algeria are the logical consequence of an abortive attempt to decerebralize a people.

One did not have to be a psychologist to divine, beneath the apparent good-nature of the Algerian, behind his stripped humility, a fundamental aspiration to dignity. And nothing is to be gained, with respect to non-simplifiable manifestations, by appealing to some form of civic conscience.

The function of a social structure is to set up institutions to serve man's needs. A society that drives its members to desperate solutions is a non-viable society, a society to be replaced.

It is the duty of the citizen to say this. No professional moral-ity, no class solidarity, no desire to wash the family linen in private, can have a prior claim. No pseudo-national mystifica-tion can prevail against the requirement of reason.

Monsieur le Ministre, the decision to punish the workers who went out on strike on July 5th, 1956, is a measure which, liter-ally, strikes me as irrational.

Either the strikers have been terrorized in their flesh and that of their families, in which case there was an obligation to under-stand their attitude, to regard it as normal, in view of the atmos-phere.

Or else their abstention expressed a unanimous current of opinion, an unshakable conviction, in which case any punitive attitude was superfluous, gratuitous, inoperative.

I owe it to the truth to say that fear has not struck me as being the dominant mood of the strikers. Rather, there was the inevitable determination to bring about, in calm and silence, a new era of peace and dignity.

The worker in the commonwealth must cooperate in the social scheme of things. But he must be convinced of the excel-lence of the society in which he lives. There comes a time when silence becomes dishonesty.

The ruling intentions of personal existence are not in accord with the permanent assaults on the most commonplace values.

For many months my conscience has been the seat of unpar-donable debates. And their conclusion is the determination not to despair of man, in other words, of myself.

The decision I have reached is that I cannot continue to bear a responsibility at no matter what cost, on the false pretext that there is nothing else to be done.

For all these reasons I have the honor, Monsieur le Ministre, to ask you to be good enough to accept my resignation and to put an end to my mission in Algeria.

Yours sincerely

IV

Toward the Liberation of Africa

1

Disappointments and Illusions of French Colonialism

For twenty years the colonial peoples have been upsetting foreign domination and establishing a footing on the international scene. One after another, some slowly, others more rapidly, the old parent states withdraw from their possessions. While the colonial expeditions conform to a given and known pattern—the necessity to establish law and order among barbarians, the protection of the concessions and interests of European countries, the generous contribution of Western civilization—not enough has been said about the stereotype of means used by the parent countries to cling to their colonies.

The Franco-Algerian war, because of its size and intensity, enables us to see in close-up, by the very reason of her successive failures, the attempts made by France to maintain her domination.

The impossible collaboration

The first tactic of the colonial countries consists of basing themselves on official collaborators and feudal elements. These Algerians, who have been particularly singled out by a series of compromises, are regrouped and requested publicly to condemn "the seditious movement that disturbs the peace of the community." In 1954 and in the course of the first months of 1955, France proceeded to make a census of its faithful and loyal servants and to mobilize them. Declarations, condemnations,

El Moudjahid, No. 10, September 1957. *El Moudjahid* was the central organ of the FLN [National Liberation Front].

appeals to wisdom were drafted, published, or read over the radio.

The colonialist authorities waited confidently, then anxiously, and finally without hope for the results of these messages. Solicited anew, the servants formed the habit, unheard of until then, of declining the invitations; they avoided the official ceremonies, and often even adopted a new vocabulary.

The fact is that the revolutionary commitment proved to be more and more total and the collaborators became aware of the gigantic awakening of a people in arms.

The economic argument

In the face of the defection even of men whom they had used and dishonored in the eyes of the Algerian people, and in the face of the active hostility of the elites, the French authorities launched the second operation.

Essentially this amounted to cutting off the presumably "sound" population from the revolutionary movement.

Incapable of apprehending the real significance of the battle for liberation, France in a first stage recognized the existence of a problem which it declared to be economic and social. In the hope of silencing the voice of national dignity, it "solemnly undertook to fight poverty and to solve the housing problem." Wages were symbolically increased and investment programs announced. This treatment of a demand for national liberation as if it were a peasant uprising, or a manifestation of social discontent, resulted from a double confusion: the idea that there is no Algerian national consciousness, on the one hand, and on the other, the conviction that the promises of improvement of the living standard of the populations would suffice to bring back order and peace.

But the French authorities, using informers who were harder and harder to find and more and more costly, were somewhat baffled to learn that the movement was solid, rooted in the masses, and driven by it.

Against a united front, inhuman and cynical methods

In a second stage, and with a rare duplicity, the French administration organized the Mozabite operation, the Kabyle operation, the Jewish operation, the *harka* operation.[1] What was concretely sought was the appearance within the population of contradictory, hence counter-revolutionary currents. These operations were characterized by the exploitation of a certain number of local hostilities created by colonialism, the maintenance and the provoked intensification of cultural differences transformed into feuds between clans or, in some cases, between "races."

Mélouza and Wagram developed, to an ultimate point of cruelty, methods in which rapes and massacres ostensibly perpetrated by the FLN, clean-ups of entire *douars*,[2] were aimed at provoking the outrage of the population and the condemnation of the revolutionary movement.

The mistake common to these various maneuvers is that the French authorities obstinately overlook the fact that the FLN identifies itself with the Algerian people. The husbands of the women who had been raped were in the local FLN group. In the evening they would come down from their operational sectors to kiss their children. And the houses of the wrecked *douar* had been built by the *moudjahidines*[3] who held the surrounding mountain.

The staff headquarters, the victim of an out-of-date policy and of its lack of information as to the structure of the FLN, imagines that in the mountains anything can happen.

But the fact is that nothing happens that is not foreseen and decided.

The movements of the units conform to a strategic program

---

[1] The Mozabites, Kabyles, and Jews are minority populations of Algeria. A *harka* is a raid.—*Tr.*

[2] *douar*—a village.—*Tr.*

[3] *Moudjahidines*—plural of *moudjahid*. Fighters (originally fighters in Moslem Holy War).—*Tr.*

drawn up by the ALN general staff.[4] Every unit has a precise sector and a command post that coordinates it.

There is no FLN unit executing a more or less coherent movement that could commit massacres at random. When a company or a battalion moves out of its sector or its region, it is carrying out a command by the *wilaya* staff.[5] This is previously communicated to the various regional or area command posts, and the march is covered by the local units.

Because they had no knowledge of this, the French authorities let loose their soldiers and their *harkas* on the Algerian civilian populations.

Each time, the will to independence grew more irrepressible.

The Mozabite operation lasted only a few days. The Algerian Mozabites, mostly tradesmen, received numerous threatening letters. Raids were organized on their shops. An atmosphere of a racist character was created. This crude attempt soon failed when the FLN brought the facts to light.

The Jewish operation likewise had a racist character. It was exposed in the famous letter of the FLN addressed to the Jewish community of Algeria.

Colonialism's trump card, however, was represented by the MNA.[6] Non-existent on the national territory, Messalism in France enjoyed the enemy's unconditional support. The French on a number of occasions facilitated the transport of hundreds of Messalists and undertook to arm them. Quickly identified upon their arrival on national territory by the FLN information agency, they joined our ranks or were sentenced to death and executed for treason to the national cause and collaboration with the enemy.

A classical explanation

There was left to France only a third and last operation to resort to. Its two phases are very similar: the discovery of

---

[4] ALN—National Liberation Army.—*Tr.*
[5] *wilaya*—a military region (the Arab word for "province").—*Tr.*
[6] MNA—Algerian Nationalist Movement, a middle-of-the-road nationalist movement which refused to join forces with the FLN. Messali Hadj was the leader of the movement.—*Tr.*

foreign and more specifically communist inspiration behind the national liberation movements.

The first, spectacular phase illustrates perfectly the degree of unawareness achieved by the French governments. The Suez expedition was meant to strike the Algerian Revolution at the summit. Egypt, accused of directing the struggle of the Algerian people, was criminally bombarded. International peace, momentarily in danger, was saved by the vigorous and unequivocal attitude of the United Nations.

At the same time, however, military operations were intensified in Algeria. The FLN took the initiative throughout the territory. The great 8-day strike reaffirmed the national unanimity in the struggle and the maintenance of the objectives.

The second phase, begun, abandoned and resumed, was never carried through. The communist scarecrow was not extensively invoked. The French colonialists sensed that it was beside the mark. They were not convinced by the argument.

Thus three political operations were directed, like the parallel military operations, against the Algerian national forces. All the known methods, all the usual maneuvers, proved ineffective, inadequate, useless. Episodically, to be sure, one or the other of these operations is again launched. But the spring is broken.

Mad dreams

Finding themselves faced with the Algerian people, the French strategists are at a loss. Their classical and long-tested techniques are no longer usable.

And so for several months we have seen France flounder in a welter of surmises. The statements of its politicians often take on a prophetic tone.

Quarrels are said to be on the point of breaking out within the FLN. The military are reportedly trying to take over the control of the movement. There is talk of a very tough fight between extremists and moderates and of the Kabyles being ready to perpetrate a *coup d'état*. On top of all this, a showdown among the colonels is supposed to be imminent.

Abandoning action and fleeing realistic decisions, France in Algeria hopes, wishes, and prophesies.

Isolated on the national territory, without any contact with the Algerian people, France adopts positions that are less and less concrete, more and more illusory.

Normally, so the French governors think, the Algerians should begin to show signs of exhaustion.

Wishes are formulated, hypotheses are put forth, and in accordance with a well-known logic these are transformed into elements of reality: the members of the National Council of the Algerian Revolution are divided and the wicked military reputedly terrorize those who are in favor of negotiation. From time to time, in their distress at the ineffectiveness of their desires, the French sulk.

The FLN is criticized for its monolithic character, for its intransigence, and the Algerian people for fighting for a dead man.

But meeting reality face to face requires other techniques. The French authorities need to understand once and for all that facts cannot be eluded. Escape into the world of desires, into futile outbursts of anger, does not constitute a solution to the Franco-Algerian war.

Yes, the Algerian people, for three years now, has been monolithic. This is because the issue is exceptionally clear and simple.

National independence through armed struggle—the objectives, limits, methods, and means of the struggle are defined once and for all.

The chimera of possible dissensions shows a total absence of critical sense since of course the reality does not seem to conform to those visions or to those desires.

The FLN is not a movement inspired by demands for better hours or wages or working conditions, and bargaining of any kind is unthinkable.

The CNRA[7] does not represent a group of interests, but

---

[7] CNRA—National Committee of the Algerian Revolution.—Tr.

the politico-military general staff of a Nation fighting for its independence.

Without any grasp of reality, unable or unwilling to recognize the Algerian national will and to draw the inescapable logical conclusions, the French authorities today live under the domination of desires and prophesies.

2

Algeria Face to Face with the French Torturers

The Algerian Revolution, through the deeply human inspiration that animates it and its passionate love of freedom, has for three years been engaged in the methodical destruction of a certain number of myths.

The Algerian Revolution does of course restore its rights to national existence. It does of course testify to the people's will. But the interest and the value of our Revolution reside in the message of which it is the bearer.

The truly monstrous practices that have appeared since November 1, 1954, are surprising especially because of the extent to which they have become generalized . . . In reality, the attitude of the French troops in Algeria fits into a pattern of police domination, of systematic racism, of dehumanization rationally pursued. Torture is inherent in the whole colonialist configuration.

The Algerian Revolution, by proposing the liberation of the national territory, is aimed both at the death of this configuration and at the creation of a new society. The independence of Algeria is not only the end of colonialism, but the disappearance, in this part of the world, of a gangrene germ and of a source of epidemic.

The liberation of the Algerian national territory is a defeat for racism and for the exploitation of man; it inaugurates the unconditional reign of Justice.

El Moudjahid, No. 10, September 1957.

The real contradiction

Wars of national liberation are often presented as expressing the internal contradictions of the colonialist countries. The Franco-Algerian war, while it takes its place in an historic context characterized by the simultaneous and successive outbreak of movements of national liberation, has its own peculiarities.

Algeria, a settlement transformed by decree into metropolitan territory, has lived under police and military domination never equalled in a colonial country. This is explained first of all by the fact that Algeria has practically never laid down its arms since 1830. But above all, France is not unaware of Algeria's importance in its colonial structure, and its obstinacy and its incalculable efforts can only be explained by the certainty that Algeria's independence would very shortly bring about the crumbling of its empire.

Situated at France's gateway, Algeria reveals to the Western world in detail, and as though in slow motion, the contradiction of the colonial situation.

The calling out of the French contingent, the mobilization of several classes, the recall of the reserve officers and noncoms, the invitations to sacrifice periodically broadcast to the people, the taxes and the freezing of wages, have involved the entire French nation in this war of colonial reconquest.

The generalized, and sometimes truly bloody enthusiasm that has marked the participation of the French workers and peasants in the war against the Algerian people has shaken to its foundations the myth of an effective opposition between the people and the government.

According to a significant statement made by one of the French prime ministers, the Nation has identified itself with its army fighting in Algeria.

The war in Algeria is being waged conscientiously by all Frenchmen and the few criticisms expressed up to the present time by a few individuals mention only certain methods which "are precipitating the loss of Algeria." But the colonial reconquest in its essence, the armed expedition, the attempt to throttle the liberty of a people, are not condemned.

Torture as a fundamental necessity of the colonial world

For some time there has been a great deal of talk about tortures applied by French soldiers to Algerian patriots. Abundant, detailed, frightful texts have been published. Historical comparisons have been made. Leading foreigners, and Frenchmen with them, have condemned these practices.

The Frenchmen who cry out against torture, or deplore its extension, inevitably remind one of those sensitive souls described by a certain philosopher, and the label of "tired intellectuals" that their compatriots Lacoste and Lejeune attach to them is very pertinent. One cannot both be in favor of the maintenance of French domination in Algeria and opposed to the means that this maintenance requires.

Torture in Algeria is not an accident, or an error, or a fault. Colonialism cannot be understood without the possibility of torturing, of violating, or of massacring.

Torture is an expression and a means of the occupant-occupied relationship.

The French police agents, who for a long time were the only ones to practice such tortures, are quite aware of this. The necessity to legitimize tortures has always been considered by them to be an outrage and a paradox.

Torture as a way of life

The fact remains that the system has accidents, breakdowns. It is of extreme importance to analyze these.

In the course of the first quarter of 1956, cases of insanity among police agents became frequent.

The disturbances that they manifested in the home (threatening to kill their wives, inflicting severe injuries on their children, insomnia, nightmares, continual threats of suicide[1]) and professional misconduct (coming to blows with colleagues, neglect of duty, lack of energy, disrespectful attitudes toward

---

[1] In Constantinois, a police officer committed suicide in 1956.

their superiors) often required medical attention, assignment to a different service or, more frequently, a transfer back to France.

The multiple appearance of dynamic revolutionary bodies, the lightning reactions of our *fidayines*,[2] the spread of the FLN throughout the national territory, confronted the French police with insurmountable problems. The permanent alert that the FLN imposed on them seemed to account for the irritability of the police.

The police have their own ready explanations.

They hit their children hard, for they think they are still with Algerians.

They threaten their wives, for "I threaten and execute all day long."

They do not sleep, because they hear the cries and the moans of their victims.

Such facts obviously create certain problems. Are these men tortured by remorse?

Is what we witness here a revolt of moral conscience?

Are the tortures admitted by these police agents exceptions?

Does the existence of these police agents on the verge of the pathological indicate the exceptional, unusual, in fact illegal character of torture?

In other words, is the police agent who exercises torture in contradiction with the "values" of his group and of the system he defends?

After having denied the existence of tortures in Algeria, the French have used a double argument.

First of all, it was claimed, the cases are exceptional.

The most serious abdication of the French intellectuals is having tolerated this lie. Sanctions will be applied, the French Government declared, but we must not make them public. As though the torture of a man or an organized massacre did not both come under public criminal law. The passion for truth and justice cannot, without challenge, accept such fraud.

---

[2] *Fidayines*—plural of *fidaï*. Death volunteers, in the Islamic tradition.—*Tr.*

The flight from responsibilities

But as the accounts of witnesses become more and more numerous, and the tortures proved themselves to be less and less exceptional, the whole responsibility was put on foreign elements serving in the French Army. This second argument is an important one. It shows both the cynicism of the French authorities and the growing impossibility of cheating, of dissimulating, of lying. The French, for one whole year, have constantly repeated that only former S.S. soldiers serving in the Foreign Legion are responsible for the tortures. As a matter of fact, the majority of the deserters from the French army are foreign legionnaires. It is because they find French police methods revolting that these Germans and these Italians abandon the enemy ranks and join the units of the ALN. We have questioned them by the scores before their repatriation. These former legionnaires all say the same thing: the cruelty and the sadism of the French forces are frightful.

In any case it is important not to forget that it was in 1955 that the soldiers began to practice torture. For nearly a year, only police agents engaged in the practice in Algeria.

Today we have detailed information on the methods used by the French. Abundant testimony has been published and the wide range of techniques has been inventoried. No material, however, has appeared on the doctrine, the philosophy of torture. Information which has reached the FLN casts a revealing light on this rationalization.

Lofrédo and Podevin, theoreticians of torture

The French police agents Lofrédo (superintendent in Algiers) and Podevin (head of the Blida judicial police) have defined, for the benefit of their friends and in the course of technical briefings to their new colleagues, certain characteristics of their methods.

1. Several converging reports by informers point to an Algerian as playing an important role in the local FLN organiza-

tion. The patriot is arrested and taken to the local judicial police headquarters. He is asked no question for, at this point in the investigation, "we do not know what direction the questioning is to take and the suspect must not suspect that we do not know." The best way is to break down his resistance by using the so-called "conditioning by example" method.

A few jeeps leave headquarters and bring back some ten Algerians picked up at random in the street or, more frequently, in a nearby *douar*. One after another, in the presence of the suspect who is the only one of interest to the police, these men are going to be tortured to death. It is felt that after five or six such murders the real questioning can begin.

2. The second method consists in first torturing the man concerned. Several sessions are needed to break down his energy. No question is asked of the suspect. Inspector Podevin, who has used this method extensively in Blida and then in Algiers, admits that it is difficult not to say anything when the tortured asks for explanations. It is therefore necessary to break down his resistance fast.

At the sixth or seventh session, he is simply told: we're listening to you.

The questioning here is not directed. The suspect is supposed to tell everything he knows.

In both cases we find the same phenomenon: the questioning is deferred.

In this perspective, in which the excuse of the end tends more and more to become detached from the means, it is normal for torture to become its own justification. And the colonialist system, in order to be logical, must be prepared to claim torture as one of its important elements.

French intellectuals and the French press

M. Martin-Chauffier, in a cautious report in which it is not difficult to discover a semi-approbation, is unable to escape this dilemma. The argument of exceptional torture is here taken up again with special vigor. The author, however, comes to recognize that, "committed at a lower echelon, these crimes are in a sense covered by the failure of the higher authorities to concern themselves sufficiently with them and, because of the virtual impunity that encourages them, threaten to become a regular system." The contradiction here is hardly deniable and in the following sentence an I.G.A.M.E., the highest French authority in Algeria, approves, advises, and legitimizes these crimes. The pretended ignorance of the higher authorities is a lie and a duplicity.

M. Martin-Chauffier would be very much surprised to learn that his attitude is considered incomprehensible here. In point of fact, torture is not a means of obtaining information. Torture is practiced in Algeria through sadistic perversion and this is the only true thing said in M. Martin-Chauffier's report: "This system has the effect of perverting those who become its instruments."

G. M. Mattei, who has participated in the French expeditions in Algeria, has just published some pages in the July-August issue of *Les Temps Modernes*. "I remember," he writes, "that from time to time, when the traveling cinema of the battalion came and showed us a film, and it didn't go over, soldiers and officers would get up and tranquilly spend the rest of the evening in the company of the prisoners . . . The screams were partly drowned by the music of the film."

M. Mattei is outraged at such violation of French dignity and honor. And, naturally, he concludes his testimony with what has become the classic argument of French democrats: "How are your youngsters going to turn out, in the cultural milieu that Algeria has become . . . ?" For the "most distressing thing," to be sure, "was what those young recruits with whom I spent six months had turned into after twelve months of overseas service —regular mercenaries."

No better example can be found of what must after all be called a perversion of the moral sense. When the French intellectuals, along with M. Mattei, repeat in chorus "that there is at the present time a vast campaign of dehumanization of French

youth," or deplore the fact that the French recruits "are learning fascism," one cannot fail to note that only the moral consequences of these crimes on the soul of the French are of concern
to these humanists. The gravity of the tortures, the horror of
the rape of little Algerian girls, are perceived because their existence threatens a certain idea of French honor.

This attitude is worth meditating. Such shutting out of the
Algerian, such ignoring of the tortured man or of the massacred
family, constitute a wholly original phenomenon. It belongs to
that form of egocentric, sociocentric thinking which has become
the characteristic of the French.

In reality, it seems that the fear of a moral (?) contamination
is quite unfounded. The sick police agents were not tormented
by their consciences. If they continue their professional practices outside their offices or their workshops—which happen to
be torture rooms—it is because they are victims of overwork.
What these police agents were looking for was not so much a
moral assuagement as the possibility of resuming the tortures.

What about the system?

The police agent who tortures an Algerian infringes no law.
His act fits into the framework of the colonialist institution. By
torturing, he manifests an exemplary loyalty to the system. And
indeed the French soldiers can hardly do otherwise without
condemning French domination. Every Frenchman in Algeria
must behave like a torturer. Wanting to remain in Algeria,
there is no other solution for France than the maintenance of a
permanent military occupation and of a powerful police structure.

The enemy forces cannot imagine how impossible it is for
them to do anything but evacuate the national territory.

The Algerian people are not fighting against tortures, the
rape of little girls, or collective murders. The history of the
French occupation is studded with such crimes, and in Kabylia,
even recently, the name of Bugeaud was used to frighten children.

The Algerian people are not unaware of the fact that the colonialist structure rests on the necessity of torturing, raping, and committing massacres.

And for this reason the demand that we make—our objective—is from the outset total and absolute.

The sadistic police agents who have lost sleep and the torturing soldiers who "run the danger of turning into fascists" present for us Algerians a precise problem. How can we modify our strategy and intensify our combat in order that the national territory may be liberated at the earliest possible moment?

Any other consideration is radically foreign to us.

3

Concerning a Plea

Looking beyond the collective executions and the torture rooms French democrats at times address themselves to the Algerian people and ask them not to embrace the different elements that represent the French people with the same contempt and with the same hatred.

Mr. Georges Arnaud recalls, not without bitterness, that everything in Algeria, and in the first place the sentencing to death of an innocent woman driven mad by her torturers, is being done in the name of the people of France.

Georges Arnaud, you must know that for three years the Algerian people have been massacred in the name of the French people.

Your plea for Djamila Bouhired honors you, but you should be told that it leaves aside the essential. The murder of Djamila Bouhired does not present any problem for the Algerian people.

Djamila Bouhired's laughter on hearing the announcement of her death sentence is neither sterile bravado nor unconsciousness—let there be no misunderstanding as to this.

That smile is rather the quiet manifestation of an inner certainty that has remained unshakable. The Algerian people gave no sign of surprise on learning of Djamila Bouhired's death sentence. For there is not one Algerian family that has not been hurt, bereaved, decimated in the name of the people of France.

Djamila Bouhired's message belongs in the tradition of Algerians who have given their lives for an independent Algeria.

El Moudjahid, No. 12, Nov. 15, 1957, on the subject of the book by Georges Arnaud and Jacques Vergès: *Pour Djamila Bouhired*.

The soldiers of the National Army, the men and women of Algeria, are enlisted, like Djamila Bouhired, in an implacable combat against foreign domination.

Georges Arnaud, there have since been a multitude of Djamila Bouhireds, tortured, violated, and massacred on Algerian territory.

There will be others and the Algerian people know it. They know that the hope of French colonialism is to shatter the national will by these executions.

The characteristic of the majority of French democrats is precisely that it experiences alarm only in connection with individual cases that are just fit to wrench a tear or to provoke little pangs of conscience.

We can measure herein the historic belatedness of the French conscience. After the fruitful struggle that it waged two centuries ago for the respect of individual liberties and the rights of man, it finds itself today unable to wage a similar battle for the rights of peoples. This explains the feverish concentration on individual cases and the vain hope of stirring the interest of the French people in the whole problem on the basis of extreme situations.

The extreme situation is neither Bouhired, nor Zeddour, nor even the Philippeville stadium.

The extreme situation is the will of twelve million men. That is the only reality. And it cannot be simplified.

Do you really think, Georges Arnaud, that you are rendering a service to the French people by speaking to them of Djamila Bouhired? Should it even happen that Djamila Bouhired was pardoned (for what?) and amnestied, would the struggle of the Algerian people and the repression carried out in the name of the French people change in form?

It is true that your book has been written for French readers. It is also true that for some time now fascist habits have manifested themselves in France, of which writers who respect themselves are bearing the brunt. Because of all this, what you have done shows courage.

The main thing, you see, is not to mix everything up. It does no good to present Djamila Bouhired as a poor girl who is the victim of wickedness.

Djamila Bouhired is a conscious Algerian patriot, organized within the FLN.

She asks neither for commiseration nor for pity. Djamila Bouhired's dignity, her extraordinary fortitude, her obstinate determination to remain upright, not to speak, her need to smile in the face of death, constitute the essential characteristics of the national attitude of the Algerian people.

Djamila Bouhired's death—and there you are right, Georges Arnaud—does constitute a problem for the French people.

We must nevertheless recognize that it does not seem that this people has perceived the frightful responsibility that it has assumed in the past four years before the world and before history in endorsing, in participating in this Algerian war, about which it has been said that it is the greatest shame of our period.

Maître Jacques Vergès was not allowed to act as Djamila Bouhired's defense lawyer. You say, Georges Arnaud, that he came close to being lynched by that part of the French people that rules in Algiers.

So we have here a new pretext for revolt: the rights of defense, the protection of defense . . .

How far we are from this war which, it will sooner or later have to be recognized, concerns two peoples.

As for Jacques Vergès, a native of Réunion, the French colony, we need only remember how several of us were trampled underfoot in Lyon ten years ago to feel on an equal footing with him.

Ten years ago hundreds of Algerian workers and students manifesting their solidarity with a relative of Maître Vergès, who was the victim of a plot in Réunion, were clubbed by the French police and *gendarmerie*.

Is it so far from Réunion to Algiers?

4

French Intellectuals and Democrats
and the Algerian Revolution

I

One of the first duties of intellectuals and democratic elements in colonialist countries is unreservedly to support the national aspirations of colonized peoples. This attitude is based on very important theoretical considerations: the defense of an idea of man challenged in the Western countries, the refusal to participate institutionally in the degradation and the negation of certain values, the community of interests between the working classes of the conquering country and the combined population of the conquered and dominated country, and finally the feeling that the government must be made to respect the right of peoples to self-determination.

This support and this solidarity find their expression, before the period of armed struggle, in the holding of a few meetings and in the adoption of motions. Sometimes, when a suddenly very fierce repression occurs, which is an obvious forerunner of a more thoroughgoing, more extensive repression (in the case of Algeria, M. Naegelen's election and the 1950-1951 plot), a press campaign, statements, warnings, appeals are prepared.

It must be pointed out that not a single attempt at an explanation is undertaken on the level of the population of the colonialist country. Because it has no hold on the people, the democratic Left, shut in upon itself, convinces itself in endless articles and studies that Bandung has sounded the death-knell

This series of three articles appeared in *El Moudjahid* in the issues of December 1, 15, and 30, 1957.

76

of colonialism. But it is the real people, the peasants and the workers, who must be informed. Incapable of reaching the millions of workers and peasants of the colonialist people and of explaining and commenting on the realities of the drama that is beginning, the Left finds itself reduced to the role of a Cassandra. It announces cataclysms, but because public opinion has not been adequately prepared, these prophesies, inexplicable in the pre-insurrectional period, will, at the time of the explosion, be regarded as proof of complicity.

A painful ineffectiveness

Thus, in the special case of Algeria, after the acute pre-insurrectional phase (1952-1953), when the period of the armed phase began (sabotaging, raids), the Left was paradoxically caught off its guard and proved helpless.

The French democratic elements and intellectuals are familiar with the problem. Having seen it at close range and having studied it for a long time, they know its complexity, its depth, and its tension. But all this knowledge proves futile because it is utterly disproportionate to the simple ideas current among the people.

Encumbered by this unusable knowledge, the Left enjoys the status of a prophet. For a long time it has repeated to those who govern: "You were forewarned; all this is happening through no fault but your own."

In this effervescent phase of alignment of forces and of organization of the armed struggle of the colonized people, we witness a partial communication between the people in revolt and the democratic elements. This is because very often the intellectuals and the democrats have personally known the present leaders of the armed struggle. There thus develops between them a kind of apparent complicity. But this active pseudo-solidarity is very quickly swept away by events. In the course of the second period, characterized by engagements, ambushes, and assaults, the guilt so generously projected onto the official heads tends in fact to be displaced. The repression goes deeper, becomes organized, diversified. Torture chambers appear. Over the whole Algerian national territory tens and hundreds of patriots are murdered.

The real people, the men and the women, the children and the old people in the colonized country, take it for granted that existing, in the biological sense of the word, and existing as a sovereign people are synonymous. The only possible issue, the sole way of salvation for this people is to react as energetically as it can to the genocide campaign being conducted against it.

The reaction is becoming progressively more absolute.

Nationalism and "barbarism"

Here we encounter a double phenomenon. First of all an ultra-chauvinistic, nationalistic, patriotic propaganda, mobilizing the implicit racist elements of the collective consciousness of the colonialist people, introduces a new element. It immediately becomes obvious that it is no longer possible to back the colonized without at the same time opposing the national solution. The fight against colonialism becomes a fight against the nation. The war of reconquest is assumed by the colonialist country as a whole, and anti-colonialist arguments lose their efficacy, become abstract theories and finally disappear from the democratic literature.

In the case of Algeria, it was after March 1955, with the calling out of the contingent, that the French nation took over the war of colonial reconquest. The demonstrations of the draftees were at that point the last symptoms of a war whose doctrinal motivations had no popular support.

From 1956 onward the Algerian war was accepted by the nation. France wants the war, as Mr. Guy Mollet and Mr. Bourgès-Maunoury have explicity stated; and the people of Paris, on July 14th, 1957, conveyed to Massu's parachutist torturers the country's deep gratitude. The liberals abandoned the struggle at this stage. The accusation of treason to which the adversaries of the Algerian war exposed themselves became a formidable weapon in the hands of the French government. Thus in early 1957 many democrats ceased their protests or were overwhelmed by the clamor for vengeance, and a clumsily structured elementary patriotism manifested itself, steeped in racism—violent, totalitarian, in short, fascist.

The French government was to find its second argument in what is called terrorism. Bombs in Algiers have been exploited by the propaganda service. Innocent children who got hurt, who did not answer to the name of Borgeaud or who did not fit the classic definition of the "ferocious colonialist," created unexpected problems for French democrats. The Left was staggered; Sakamody accentuated this reaction. Ten French civilians, in this case, were killed in an ambush and the entire French Left, in a unanimous outburst, cried out: we can no longer follow you! The propaganda became orchestrated, wormed its way into people's minds and dismantled convictions that were already crumbling. The concept of barbarism appeared and it was decided that France in Algeria was fighting barbarism.

A large proportion of the intellectuals, almost the entire democratic Left, collapsed and laid down its conditions before the Algerian people: condemn Sakamody and the bombs and we shall continue to give you our friendly support.

On the dawn of the fourth year of the war of national liberation, in the face of the French nation and in the face of the bombs that had been exploded on the rue Michelet, the French Left was more and more conspicuous by its absence.

Some took refuge in silence; others chose certain themes, which reappear periodically. The Algerian war must end for it is too costly (the Algerian war is again becoming unpopular, simply because it costs 1200 billion francs), it isolates France or makes possible her replacement by the Anglo-Saxons or by the Russians or by Nasser, etc. . . .

In France it becomes less and less clear why the Algerian war must end. People forget more and more that France, in Algeria, is trampling popular sovereignty underfoot, flouting the right of peoples to self-determination, murdering thousands of men and women.

In France, among the Left, the Algerian war is tending to

become a disease of the French system, like ministerial instability, and colonial wars a nervous tic with which France is
afflicted, a part of the national panorama, a familiar detail.

II

Since 1956, French intellectuls and democrats have periodically addressed themselves to the FLN. Most of the time they
have proffered either political advice or criticisms concerning
this or that aspect of the war of liberation. This attitude of the
French intelligentsia must not be interpreted as the consequence of an inner solidarity with the Algerian people. This
advice and these criticisms are to be explained by the ill-re-
pressed desire to guide, to direct the very liberation movement
of the oppressed.

Thus can be understood the constant oscillation of the
French democrats between a manifest or latent hostility and the
wholly unreal aspiration to militate "actively to the end." Such
a confusion indicates a lack of preparation for the facing of
concrete problems and a failure on the part of French democrats
to immerse themselves in the political life of their own country.

Along this oscillating line the French democrats—outside the
struggle or intent upon observing it from within, and even participating in it in the capacity of censors, of advisers, unable or
refusing to choose a precise ground on which to fight within the
French system—issue threats and practice blackmail.

The pseudo-justification for this attitude is that in order to
have an influence on French public opinion, certain facts must
be condemned, the unexpected excrescences must be rejected,
the "excesses" must be disavowed. In these moments of crisis, of
face-to-face opposition, the FLN is being asked to direct its
violence, and to make it selective.

The myth of French Algeria

At this level, reflection enables us to discover an important
peculiarity of colonial reality in Algeria. Within a nation it is

usual and commonplace to identify two antagonistic forces: the working class and bourgeois capitalism. In a colonial country this distinction proves totally inadequate. What defines the colonial situation is rather the undifferentiated character that foreign domination presents. The colonial situation is first of all a military conquest continued and reinforced by a civil and police administration. In Algeria, as in every colony, the foreign oppressor looks upon the native as marking a limit to his dignity and defines himself as constituting an irreducible negation of the colonized country's national existence.

The status of the foreigner, of the conqueror, of the Frenchman in Algeria, is the status of an oppressor. The Frenchman in Algeria cannot be neutral or innocent. Every Frenchman in Algeria oppresses, despises, dominates. The French Left, which cannot remain indifferent and impervious to its own phantasms, adopted paradoxical positions in Algeria, during the period preceding the war of liberation.

What is colonialism?

French democrats, in deciding to give the name of "colonialism" to what has never ceased to be military conquest and occupation, have deliberately simplified facts. The term of colonialism created by the oppressor is too affective, too emotional. It is placing a national problem on a psychological level. This is why, as conceived by these democrats, the contrary of colonialism is not the recognition of the right of peoples to self-determination, but the necessity, on an individual level, for less racist, more open, more liberal types of behavior.

Colonialism is not a type of individual relations but the conquest of a national territory and the oppression of a people: that is all. It is not a certain type of human behavior or a pattern of relations between individuals. Every Frenchman in Algeria is at the present time an enemy soldier. So long as Algeria is not independent, this logical consequence must be accepted. Mr. Lacoste shows that he has understood it, by his "surface mobilization" of the Frenchmen and Frenchwomen residing in Algeria.

At the end of this analysis we perceive that, far from reproaching the National Liberation Front for some of its urban actions, we should on the contrary appreciate the efforts that it imposes on the people.

It is because they have failed to understand that colonialism is only military domination that the French democrats have reached a paradoxical extreme.

Victims of the myth of French Algeria, the parties of the Left create Algerian sections of the French political parties on Algerian territory. The slogans, the programs, the methods of struggle are identical to those of the "metropolis." A doctrinal position, unchallenged until just recently, has justified this attitude. In a colonial country, it used to be said, there is a community of interests between the colonized people and the working class of the colonialist country. The history of the wars of liberation waged by the colonized peoples is the history of the non-verification of this thesis.

Colonialism is not Mr. Borgeaud

The Algerian people has proved refractory to the over-simple imagery according to which the colonialist is a special type of man who can be readily recognized. Thus it has been claimed that all Frenchmen in Algeria are not colonialists, and that there are different degrees of colonialism. Now neither Mr. Borgeaud nor Mr. de Sérigny wholly characterize French colonialism in Algeria. French colonialism, French oppression in Algeria, form a coherent whole which does not necessarily require the existence of Mr. Borgeaud. French domination is the totality of the forces that are opposed to the existence of the Algerian nation, and for the Algerian, concretely, Mr. Blachette is no more "colonialist" than a police officer, a rural policeman, or a school teacher.

The Algerian experiences French colonialism as an undifferentiated whole, not out of simplemindedness or xenophobia but because in reality every Frenchman in Algeria maintains, with reference to the Algerian, relations that are based on force. The evocation of special cases of Frenchmen who are abnormally nice to Algerians does not modify the nature of the relations between a foreign group that has seized the attributes of national sovereignty and the people which finds itself deprived of the exercise of power. No personal relation can contradict this fundamental datum: that the French nation through its citizens opposes the existence of the Algerian nation.

In colonies that are held solely by occupying forces, the colonial people is represented by the soldiers, the police, and the technicians. Under those conditions the colonialist people can take refuge in ignorance of the facts and claim to be innocent of the colonization. In settlement colonies, on the other hand, this running away from oneself becomes impossible. Because, in accordance with the famous formula of a French chief of state, "there is not a single Frenchman who does not have a cousin in Algeria," the whole French nation finds itself involved in the crime against a people and is today an accomplice in the murders and the tortures that characterize the Algerian war.

The authentic French democrat cannot just be *against* Mr. Borgeaud or Mr. Blachette; he must avoid choosing arbitrarily a few scapegoats who cannot express the 130 years of colonialist oppression. The French democrat must judge and condemn colonization as a whole in its category of military and police oppression. He must convince himself that every Frenchman in Algeria reacts as Mr. Borgeaud does. Because there is not a Frenchman in Algeria who is not justified in his very existence by this domination.

Unable to adopt this attitude, through lack of courage or failure of analysis, the French democrat is constantly resorting to abstractions as points of reference: colonialism in general is dying, colonialism is inhuman, France must remain faithful to its history, thus pointedly forgetting that colonialism constitutes an important part of French history.

Colonialism is the organization of the domination of a nation after military conquest. The war of liberation is not a seeking for reforms but the grandiose effort of a people, which had been mummified, to rediscover its own genius, to reassume its history and assert its sovereignty.

Frenchmen, within the framework of NATO, refuse to serve under the orders of the German general Speidel, but are willing to fight against the Algerian people. But strictly speaking, fidelity to the spirit of the French resistance should impel Frenchmen who find it distasteful to serve under Speidel to refuse, in terms of their own logic, to fight under Massu or Salan.

III

The men who govern France are obviously right when they claim that the Algerian problem is shaking the very foundations of the Republic. For some years the myth of French Algeria has been put to severe tests, and a dose of uncertainty has crept into the French consciousness as to the truth of this thesis.

On the international level, repercussions of this destruction have been noted. Such progress, however, has not totally solved the problem of the mystification engendered by dozens of years of wrong teaching and of systematized historic falsification.

The price of mystification

When one closely examines the colonial relations that have existed between Algeria and France one notes that the Algerian territory, by the very characteristics of the conditions of its conquest, has always represented for France a more or less real prolongation. At no time has France indicated in identical terms its property rights over Africa south of the Sahara, or over any other fragment of the "French Empire." Africa south of the Sahara may have been decreed French territory, but never was it decided that Africa south of the Sahara was France.

France's right in Africa was based rather on a right of property, whereas in Algeria, from the beginning, relations of identity were affirmed. We have seen that French democrats, with rare exceptions, have adapted their attitude to this view. French political parties have not concealed the necessity they felt to mark obedience to this mystification. Mr. Laurent Casanova, in a speech to the Communist students delivered on March 17, 1957 in Paris, in response to criticisms leveled at him by the Communist youth on the attitude of the French Communist Party in respect to the Algerian problem, justified himself by asking them to take into account "the spontaneous attitude of the French popular masses on the question."

Because for 130 years the French national consciousness has been conditioned by one simple basic principle—Algeria *is* France—we today find ourselves up against instinctive, passionate, anti-historic reactions, at a moment when a large proportion of the French people rationally realizes that its interest can best be served by putting an end to the war and recognizing an independent Algerian State.

Never was the principle according to which no one can enslave another so wholly true. After having domesticated the Algerian people for more than a century, France finds herself a prisoner of her conquest and incapable of detaching herself from it, of defining new relations, of making a fresh start.

A hateful deal

It would be a great mistake, however, to believe the problem to be exhausted by these psychological considerations. The encounters with the representatives of the French Left bring out much more complex concerns. Thus, on the precise point of the future of independent Algeria, we face two contradictory demands which, incidentally, match at a higher level the Manichean conception of good and evil that for some years now has divided the world.

The non-Communist Left assures us of its support, promises to act in our behalf, but asks us to give our guarantee that Algeria will never fall into the Communist bloc or into the so-called neutralist bloc. The anti-colonialism of these democrats is therefore not unreserved and unconditional, but assumes a precise political choice. They do not lack arguments, to be sure. Exchanging French colonialism for a red or Nasserian "colonialism" appears to them to be a negative operation, for, they claim, at the present historic hour of great combinations, an alignment is compulsory and there is nothing veiled about their advice: one must choose the Western bloc.

This non-Communist Left is generally reticent when we explain to them that, for the moment, the Algerian people must first of all liberate itself from the French colonialist yoke. Refusing to confine itself to the strict ground of decolonization and national liberation, the French non-Communist Left implores us to combine the two efforts: rejection of French colonialism and of Soviet-neutralist communism.

The same problem, in obedience to an opposite dynamism, arises with the French Communist Left. The French Communist Party, it says, can support only certain national liberation movements, for what would be the advantage, for us French Communists, of having American imperialism take over Algeria? Here again guarantees are demanded of us. Pressure is put upon us to give promises, assurances.

It will be understood that such difficulties stand in the way of the anti-colonialist action of the French Left. This is because the not yet independent Algeria has already become a bone of contention on an international scale. For whom, indeed, is Algeria going to be liberated? For three years the Algerian people has not ceased repeating that it proposes to liberate itself for its own sake, that what is important for it is first of all to reconquer its sovereignty, to establish its authority, to achieve its humanization, its economic and political freedom; but these obvious objectives do not seem to find acceptance.

The Algerian people is undergoing its birth to independence in the midst of terrifying suffering and already the slightest bit of support is being haggled over with unaccustomed aggressiveness. Thus it is not rare to hear certain democratic Frenchmen tell us: help us to help you. Which clearly means: give us some idea of which direction you expect to take afterwards.

This summons, which is always proffered on an individual level between Frenchmen and Algerians, certainly represents one of the most painful aspects of the struggle for independence. Certain French democrats are at times shocked by the sincerity of the Algerian fighter. This is because the total character of the war that we wage has a repercussion on the no less radical manner in which we conduct individual exchanges. And we must confess that it is unendurably painful for us to see certain Frenchmen whom we had considered our friends behave with us like tradesmen and practice this kind of hateful blackmail whereby solidarity is hedged about with all sorts of fundamental restrictions as to our objectives.

A fundamental disagreement

If we examine the attitude of the French Left with respect to the objectives of our struggle, we perceive that no faction admits the possibility of a real national liberation.

The non-Communist Left concedes that the colonial status must disappear. But, between the liquidation of the colonial system—reduced under the circumstances to a preferential system, with a struggle of castes within a whole—and the recognition of an Algerian nation, independent of France, this Left has interposed a multitude of stages, of sub-stages, of original solutions, or compromises.

It is clear that for this part of the Left the end of the Algerian war must bring about a kind of international federalism and of renovated French Union. Our disagreement with this French opinion is thus neither of a psychological order nor of a tactical order, as some pretend. The Left-wing radicals, the minority socialists, and the Left wing of the MRP[1] have not accepted the idea of an Algerian independence. There is therefore something radically false about positions that begin with the formula: "We agree in substance but not as to the methods ..."

The Communist Left, for its part, while proclaiming the necessity for colonial countries to evolve toward independence, requires the maintenance of special links with France. Such positions clearly manifest that even the so-called extremist parties consider that France has rights in Algeria and that the lightening of domination does not necessarily imply the disap-

[1] MRP—Popular Republican Movement, the French Catholic party.—*Tr.*

pearance of every link. This mental attitude assumes the guise of a technocratic paternalism, of a disingenuous warning against the danger of regression.

After breaking all links with France, it is argued, what will you do?

You need technicians, currency, machines . . .

Not even the catastrophic prospect of an Algeria consumed by the desert, infested by marshes, and ravaged by disease, is spared us in the campaign to give us pause.

The colonialists tell the French people in their propaganda: France cannot live without Algeria.

The French anti-colonialists say to the Algerians: Algeria cannot live without France.

The French democrats do not always perceive the colonialist, or—to use a new concept—the neo-colonialist character of their attitude.

The demand for special links with France is a response to the desire to maintain colonial structures intact. What is involved here is a kind of terrorism of necessity on the basis of which it is decided that nothing valid can be conceived or achieved in Algeria independently of France. In fact, the demand for special links with France comes down to a determination to maintain Algeria eternally in a stage of a minor and protected State. But also to a determination to guarantee certain forms of exploitation of the Algerian people. It is unquestionably proof of a grave failure to understand the revolutionary implications of the national struggle.

Is it too late?

The French democrats must rise above the contradictions that sterilize their positions if they wish to achieve an authentic democratization with the colonialists. It is to the extent to which French democratic opinion is without reticences that its action can be effective and decisive.

Because the Left unconsciously obeys the myth of French Algeria, its action does not go beyond aspiring to an Algeria in which more justice and freedom would prevail or, at most, an Algeria less directly governed by France. The passion-charged chauvinism of French public opinion on the Algerian question exerts pressure on this Left, inclines it to excessive caution, shakes its principles, and places it in a paradoxical and increasingly sterile situation.

The Algerian people considers that the French Left has not done everything it should within the framework of the Algerian war. It is not up to us to accuse the French democrats, but we feel duty-bound to draw their attention to certain attitudes that appear to us to be contrary to the principles of anti-colonialism.

It is perhaps worth recalling the attitude of the Socialist International on this question. No one has forgotten that in 1956 the French delegation led by Mr. Pineau was condemned by the International and that Mr. Bevan in 1957, at the Socialist Congress of Toulouse, publicly expressed his disappointment and his anger at the racism and the colonialism manifested by the SFIO.[2]

Since 1954 the Algerian people has been fighting for national independence. What is involved is a territory conquered more than a century ago which expresses its will to set itself up as a sovereign nation. The French Left should unreservedly support this effort. Neither the presence of a European minority, nor Sakamody, can or should affect the determination of an authentic Left. We have seen that Mr. Lacoste's propaganda keeps affirming that France, in Algeria, is fighting barbarism. The Left must prove itself immune to this campaign and demand the end of the war and the recognition of Algeria's independence.

It has happened, as we have seen, that certain democrats resort to the following reasoning: if you wish our aid to continue, condemn such and such acts. Thus the struggle of a people for its independence must be diaphanous if it would enjoy the support of democrats.

Here, paradoxically, may be recognized the attitude of Mr.

---

[2] SFIO—*Section Française de l'Internationale Ouvrière,* the French Socialist Party.—*Tr.*

Guy Mollet who, in order to continue his war, appoints a safe-guard commission assigned to call attention to "excesses," thus spectacularly isolating the bad soldiers from the good and true and fertile French army.

The tasks of the French Left

The FLN addresses itself to the entire French Left and asks of it, in this fourth year, to become concretely involved in the fight for peace in Algeria.

There can be no question, at any moment, of French democrats joining our ranks or betraying their country. Without renouncing their nation, the French Left must fight to make the government of their country respect the values which we call the right of peoples to self-determination, recognition of the national will, liquidation of colonialism, mutual and enriching relations among free peoples.

The FLN addresses itself to the French Left, to French democrats, and asks them to encourage every strike undertaken by the French people against the rise in the cost of living, new taxes, the restriction of democratic freedoms in France, all of which are direct consequences of the Algerian war.

The FLN asks the French Left to strengthen its action in spreading information and to continue to explain to the French masses the characteristics of the struggle of the Algerian people, the principles that animate it, the objectives of the Revolution.

The FLN salutes the French who have had the courage to refuse to take up arms against the Algerian people and who are now in prison.

These examples must be multiplied in order that it may become clear to everyone and first of all to the French government that the French people refuses this war which is being waged in its name against the right of peoples, for the maintenance of oppression, against the reign of freedom.

5

Maghreb Blood Shall Not Flow in Vain

A little more than a year ago, when the news of the interception of the plane that carried the representatives of the FLN to the Maghreb conference in Tunis was announced, Frenchmen in the streets of Algiers or in Paris could be seen to embrace with joy and enthusiasm.

On February 8, 1958, on the eve of the arrival in Tunis of his Majesty Mohammed V, invited by President Bourguiba to discuss the Algerian question, a squadron of 25 planes let loose upon the village of Sakiet Sidi Youssef a sheaf of bombs, rockets and machine-gun bullets, killing nearly 100 civilians, wounding more than 200 and destroying nearly the whole village.

The various inroads made by French forces on Tunisian territory in the course of which scores of Tunisians lost their lives had aroused the people's indignation. At each of these inroads the Tunisians, men and women, grew increasingly conscious of the precarious character of their independence. This precariousness took root first in connection with the Franco-Algerian conflict, then with the imposition of French military forces on the national territory. President Bourguiba several times had asked the French government to open negotiations with a view to evacuating its troops, and each time the French authorities provoked incidents, created tension, and deferred the general discussion on the withdrawal of the French army. With Sakiet Sidi Youssef the Tunisian people was convinced that not only did the French mean to "punish" it for its solidarity with the Algerian people but also that they hoped to use this solidarity as a pretext for reconquering Tunisia, thereby proving once and

El Moudjahid, No. 18, February 15, 1958.

for all that the Maghreb was one and that it must be dominated by French imperialism.

This is why the Tunisians did not need to exhibit their anger or to shout their determination. In four days, in an impressive calm, the people facing its destiny, after having anticipated all the risks threatening a people that means to remain free, reached the decision that Sakiet Sidi Youssef would be the last gesture of French colonialism in Tunisia. Which means that during those four days of reflection the Tunisian men and women, once again confronted with a fundamental choice, reaffirmed their oath given several years before to root out of their country the last sequels of French colonialism. Which also means that the Tunisian people behind President Bourguiba decreed a state of emergency. The slogan, the vital principle today for the Tunisian people, is the total evacuation of the national territory by the French colonialist occupants.

Not enough thought has been given to the rigorous pairing of the two expressions most used since February 8th: "evacuation" and "weapons." The Tunisian people is quite aware of the fact that the French are not ready to leave their barracks "nicely." The Tunisians know that once again it will be necessary to push the French soldiers into the sea.

It has been said that the barriers on the road were light, that they were fragile, symbolic. The presence of hunting rifles, the disarming of young neo-Destourians, have been mockingly referred to; the French correspondents accredited to Tunis go out of their way to point up the ineffective and essentially illusory character of the measures taken by the Tunisian people. But there is one argument that is utterly worthless when applied to colonial countries. This is the argument of guns and tanks. For quite some time now the argument of authority has broken down in all colonial countries.

The Tunisian people has pledged itself before its country and before its flag not to leave the street, not to rest, before the last soldier has evacuated the national territory. This is something every Frenchman must know. It is no longer possible for for-

eign, enemy troops, who endanger the inner regime and the
foundations of the nation, to maintain themselves in the country, against the people's will.

In France many people have embraced. The French newspapers that sell over a million copies have expressed the view
that the Tunisians got no more than they deserved, that it was
too bad for Bourguiba, and that upon reflection this was only
the beginning. It must be recognized that in official circles the
first reactions expressed a certain embarrassment. Mr. Pineau
gave a famous interview with a double version, while Mr. Gaillard suddenly came down with the grippe.

But this hesitancy was rapidly to give way to the most extraordinary display of aggressiveness and of bellicosity we have
seen in a long time. Before Parliament Mr. Gaillard threw back
the responsibility on Mr. Bourguiba and Mr. Pineau did not
hesitate to threaten Tunisia with the French Toulon fleet if the
troops continued to be hindered in their movements.

In Algiers the French invited the government to pursue its
raids of reprisal and in any case were of the view that French
aviation could no longer tolerate the insults directed at its
flag.

There were people in France, to be sure, who regretted the
raid on Sakiet Sidi Youssef, but such regrets were qualified. It
was said to be an error, or a fault. Some made a point of saying
that the action had been inadvisable. Others stressed the fact
that the Red Cross must not be overlooked, etc. There were,
finally, the other regrets, the sincere ones, but their sincerity,
alas, was ineffective.

Be that as it may, what the Tunisian people demand is not
regrets. What the Tunisians, men and women, demand is not
compensation for the victims of Sakiet Sidi Youssef; men,
women and children have died under the blows of colonialism
in order that the unified Maghreb might live in independence
and freedom.

The decision of the Tunisian government to bring the crime

of Sakiet before the Security Council appropriately expresses the depth of the Tunisian will.

Since it has now been proved in the eyes of international opinion that the French army, which distinguishes itself only by pillaging or massacring civilians, intends to serve as a means of pressure on the Tunisian government by constantly threatening its national independence, it is up to the Security Council to say whether it is willing to see a foreign army occupy a country against its will.

The immense majority of world opinion has not hesitated to condemn the French aggression. The Americans, slaves of the Manichaean madness, have trembled for a week lest Tunisia "should fall into Nasserism." And American newspapermen can be seen frantically trying to find out what are the risks of such a turnabout.

Americans should be told that if they want to fight communism they must, in certain sectors, adopt Communist attitudes. For colonial peoples enslaved by Western nations, the Communist countries are the only ones that have on all occasions taken their defense. The colonialized countries need not concern themselves to find out whether this attitude is dictated by the interests of Communist strategy; they note first of all that this general behavior is to their interest.

The colonial peoples are not particularly communistic, but they are irreducibly anti-colonialist.

They will not choose the United States because they are afraid of communism, but because their attitude in the great problems that shake the world—in this case the problems of decolonization—will conform to a spirit of solidarity, of equity, and of authentic justice.

The Algerian people, whatever the weak-hearted or the weak-spirited may think, does not rejoice because Sakiet Sidi Youssef has been bombarded. We do not seek to exploit this event. We are fundamentally opposed to the policy of the greater evil. It is with grief and with sorrow that we learned of the frightful butchery of Sakiet Sidi Youssef.

No man's death is indispensable for the triumph of freedom. It happens that one must accept the risk of death in order to bring freedom to birth, but it is not lightly that one witnesses so many massacres and so many acts of ignominy. Although the Algerian people have a daily experience of the French B-26 planes, it has been shaken by the tragedy of Sakiet Sidi Youssef.

The FLN's Committee of Coordination and of Execution has offered to commit all its available troops to help the Tunisian people drive the French occupant out of Tunisia.

We maintain this offer, and we say to the Tunisian people that we are together for better and for worse, that the Maghreb blood is sufficiently generous and it offers itself in great streams to the end that from Algeria to Sfax there shall be no more French soldiers to threaten, torture, and massacre the Maghreb peoples.

6

The Farce That Changes Sides

For nearly two months we have witnessed the really frenzied attempt on the part of the Anglo-Americans to transform the tragedy of Sakiet Sidi Youssef, which is a prolongation of the greater Algerian tragedy, into a farce in which indecency blends with absurdity.

After Sakiet, Tunisia lodged a complaint against France before the Security Council. As a second step, the Tunisian Republic submitted the Algerian problem before the international body. Sakiet obliged the Tunisian people to make precise demands: the evacuation of the French troops from Bizerte, the restitution of the Tunisian airfields and, on an international level, diplomatic intervention in respect to the Algerian conflict.

The Anglo-Americans, resorting to blackmail in the name of Western solidarity, promised the Tunisian government to see to it that France respected all these points, on condition that the Communist nations be not involved in the "inner problems" of the Atlantic alliance through the intervention of the Security Council.

For a month Messrs. Murphy and Beeley have been seen to meet and to discuss. "We want to bring the French and the Tunisian points of view closer together," they claimed, and during this time the French government, shaken for a moment, resumed its bellicose argumentation. In Algeria the massacres continued and the Algerian people found itself facing 87 dead, a village razed to the ground, and obstructions that took less and less account of its suffering and its anger.

El Moudjahid, No. 21, April 1st, 1958.

The President of the Tunisian Republic made certain modifications with respect to the Tunisian people's demands. But the moment the Chief of the Tunisian government announced these concessions and defined their limits, the President of the French Council, Mr. Gaillard, presented other demands, required strict guarantees, demanded of the Tunisian people a yes or a no, in short resumed the policy of aggressiveness, of menace, of intimidation.

Now there is one point to which it may be useful to draw attention. It is the fact that Mr. Dulles was able to declare: "After the concessions made by the Tunisian government, it is up to France to speak."

We have said more than once that with colonialism it is useless to hope for the slightest softening. French colonialism is a war force; it has to be beaten down by force. No diplomacy, no political genius, no skill can cope with it. Incapable as it is of disavowing itself, the democratic forces must ally themselves to destroy it.

As for us Algerians, we have in the course of our years of struggle brought into existence a certain number of truths which have swept away the historically established lies. For us Algerians, the triumph of democracy does not depend solely on the Western world since it is actually this same Western world that challenges its values.

Messrs. Murphy and Beeley, through the subtle play of prolonged silences and a paradoxical optimism, try to create confusion in the anti-colonialist world. They must know that they may perhaps fool many people, but not the Algerian people.

Messrs. Murphy and Beeley will not transform the struggle of the Maghreb people for independence into a farce.

The Anglo-American plenipotentiaries must abandon all hope of playing with the Maghreb people like puppeteers.

It is up to the Moroccan and Tunisian peoples to oppose firmly the maneuvers of the spokesmen of the French government, delegated by the Atlantic world.

The tragedy of Sakiet, the tragedy of the genocide perpetrated in Algeria by the Western and Christian French people, shall not be transformed into a burlesque comedy in which anyone can say anything he likes, it being understood that the "strongest one" will have the last word.

It is the very theory of the traditional force of mercenary countries that sinks into ridicule.

If the farce is to be played, it will be played by France. It is France, its regime, and its people who will pay the cost.

7

Decolonization and Independence

For more than three years France has been "hanging on" in Algeria. She hangs on in the most stubborn, the most bitter way, to such a point that never, in the disastrous hours of 1940, was the memory of Clémenceau so often evoked.

France has lost her foothold in Tunisia and in Morocco, but clings to the Algerian territory. For a variety of reasons, the whole gamut of French public opinion, with rare exceptions, has honored the army, backed the war in Algeria, warned the different governments against unacceptable renunciations in Algeria.

Despite the weariness that periodically comes over the French political spheres each time Mr. Lacoste calls upon the country to gird itself for one last effort, despite a more and more alarming budgetary crisis, despite the splintering of nearly all the political parties over the Algerian war, it is surprising that no coherent and effective force has come forward to impose peace on the French colonialists.

We are always being reproached for our sharp-edged diplomacy. We are reminded that Ho Chi Minh, during the most tragic hours of the war in Indochina, never ceased to mark the difference between colonialism and the French people. Even the examples of President Bourguiba and the brothers of the Istiqlal are evoked to invite us to come to terms.

Yet it must not be forgotten, if we are going to speak of Indochina, that it was the decision to send the contingent there to supplement the volunteer forces that brought about the fall of the Laniel government, the coalition of the forces of the Left, and the Geneva meeting.

El Moudjahid, No. 22, April 16, 1958.

It is true that there was also Dien Bien Phu. But Mr. Laniel's recent book and the thundering declarations of former Indochina generals claim that, despite Dien Bien Phu, if the "liquidators" had not betrayed the nation—in other words, if they had not opposed the sending of the contingent—Indochina might have been saved.

What has to be said is that with the Algerian war there appeared three phenomena, absolutely new in the struggles for national liberation.

A demand and not a prayer

To begin with, at no moment has the FLN appealed to the generosity, to the magnanimity, to the good-nature of the colonizer. In a dizzyingly swift mutation, the colonized acquires a new quality, which develops in and through combat. The language used by the FLN, from the first days of the Revolution, is a language of authority. The appeals to the French democratic forces are not drafted in ambiguous terms having a more or less infantile tinge. We say to the French Left: be logical with yourselves—help us; support the cause of the Algerian Revolution. The FLN's constant concern to rid the relations between colonized and colonizer, between the Algerian people and the French people, of the traditional confusion has placed the French democratic elements in an unusual situation. What we ask is that their action be steeped, not in an atmosphere of diffuse sympathy, but in the doctrinal rigor of an authentic anticolonialism. Insistence on such a demarcation of frontiers might, after superficial examination, be considered rigidity. That is why it is not rare to hear French democrats retort: "If you continue, we shall let you drop." Such a position indicates that the action of the democrats is devoid of any revolutionary and doctrinal value, for it feeds on the ambivalent sources of kindness to the oppressed, or a thirst to *do* something, to be useful, etc. . . .

The FLN has been reproached for not knowing how to speak to Frenchmen, for not taking sufficient account of their little weaknesses and their narcissism. This is certainly true.

But such reproaches indicate that the objective of the FLN is virtually overlooked. The FLN does not aim at achieving a decolonization of Algeria or a relaxation of the oppressive structure.

What the FLN demands is the independence of Algeria. An independence which will allow the Algerian people to take its destiny wholly in hand.

This objective, this strategy, commands our tactics, our method, and informs the very nature of our struggle.

Colonialism is fundamentally inexcusable

The Algerian Revolution has introduced a scandal in the unfolding of the struggles for national liberation. Colonialism generally manages, at the turning-point when history and the nation will reject it, to maintain itself as a value. It is not true that it was a good thing for France to have made of Algeria what she is today.

The port of Mers El Kebir and the Boufarik airfield for jet planes will never console us for the great intellectual, moral, and material wretchedness of our people.

French colonialism will not be legitimized by the Algerian people. No spectacular undertaking will make us forget the legalized racism, the illiteracy, the flunkeyism generated and maintained in the very depth of the consciousness of our people.

This is why in our declarations there is never any mention of adaptation or of alleviation, but only of restitution. It is true that the FLN is constantly being reproached for this constant reference to the Algerian nation before Bugeaud. That is because by insisting on this national reality, by making of the Revolution of November 1st, 1954, a phase of the popular resistance begun with Abd El Kader, we rob French colonialism of its legitimacy, its would-be incorporation into Algerian reality. Instead of integrating colonialism, conceived as the birth of a new world, in Algerian history, we have made of it an unhappy, execrable accident, the only meaning of which was to have inexcusably retarded the coherent evolution of the Algerian society and nation.

The "nation in the process of becoming," "new Algeria," "the unique historic case," all these mystifying expressions have been swept away by the position of the FLN and only the heroic combat of a whole people against a century-old oppression has remained in the full sunlight.

Between the break with the Algerian past, entailing as a consequence the acceptance of a renovated but continued colonization, and fidelity to the transitorily subdued nation, the Algerian people has chosen.

There is no new entity born of colonialism. The Algerian people has refused to let the occupation be transformed into collaboration. The French in Algeria have not cohabited with the Algerian people. They have more or less dominated. This is why it was necessary from the beginning to make the French people feel the full scope of our demands.

The FLN has not played with words. It has said that its objective was independence, that no concession could be made as to that objective. The FLN has told the French that it would have to negotiate with the Algerian people, restore its country to it, its whole country.

From the very beginning, the FLN defined its program: to put an end to French occupation, to give the land to the Algerians, to establish a policy of social democracy in which man and woman have an equal right to culture, to material well-being, and to dignity.

It is a liberated individual who undertakes to build the new society

Such an attitude was soon to have important repercussions on the consciousness of the Algerian.

All the degrading and infantilizing structures that habitually infest relations between the colonized and the colonizer were suddenly liquidated. Whereas the colonized usually has only a choice between a retraction of his being and a frenzied attempt at identification with the colonizer, the Algerian has brought into existence a new, positive, efficient personality, whose richness is provided less by the trial of strength that he engages in than by his certainty that he embodies a decisive moment of the national consciousness.

The Algerian combatant is not only up in arms against the torturing parachutists. Most of the time he has to face problems of building, of organizing, of inventing the new society that must come into being. That is why colonialism has lost, has irreversibly lost the battle in Algeria. In every *wilaya*, cadastral plans are drawn up, school building plans studied, economic reconversions pursued.

The Algerian builds, organizes, legislates, plans. Whence his assurance, his firm and resolute language, the energetic cohesion of his positions.

One understands why the spokesmen for the FLN are generally described as uncompromising. It is not the tone that indisposes but the content of our demands.

Many colonized peoples have demanded the end of colonialism, but rarely like the Algerian people.

This refusal of progressive solutions, this contempt for the "stages" that break the revolutionary torrent and cause the people to unlearn the unshakable will to take everything into their hands at once in order that everything may change, constitutes the fundamental characteristic of the struggle of the Algerian people.

And the *moudjahid* which sets forth this position, defends it and makes it triumph, introduces a new element into the classic dialogue of the dominated and the oppressor. The liberation of the individual does not follow national liberation. An authentic national liberation exists only to the precise degree to which the individual has irreversibly begun his own liberation. It is not possible to take one's distance with respect to colonialism without at the same time taking it with respect to the idea that the colonized holds of himself through the filter of colonialist culture.

Such a revolution on the scale of national consciousness and of individual consciousness needed to be analyzed. It enables one to understand the disintegration and the fear of French colonialism in Algeria.

The Algerian revolution introduces a new style into the struggles for national liberation

There is a third phenomenon not yet identifiable but which in its overtones, plays havoc with the relations of all the colonized with France. The process of liberation of colonial peoples is indeed inevitable. But the form given to the struggle of the Algerian people is such, in its violence and in its total character, that it will have a decisive influence on the future struggles of the other colonies.

The Algerian people is experiencing concretely the interdependence of historic phenomena. To say that the localized collapse of colonialism increases its disintegration as a system is no longer the explanation of an abstract principle which is perceptible only to intellectuals.

The whole Algerian people knows that after Algeria it will be the turn of Africa south of the Sahara to wage its fight. And is it not true that even now France finds herself reduced to inventing new formulae, to voting the *Loi-Cadre*[1] and then going beyond it, moving in spite of herself in the direction of recognition of the national sovereignty of Africa south of the Sahara?

There are, to be sure, African political men who are prisoners of the French and who try to follow the irresistible curve of the national movement.

Up to the present they have managed to adopt the different positions of their peoples with sufficient promptness. But sooner or later the divorce will manifest itself. They will then have to be "traitors" in broad daylight or abandon the mirages of colonizing work.

The Algerian people knows that the peoples of Africa south of the Sahara are watching its struggle against French colonial-

---

[1] *Loi-Cadre*, a law which defines a certain principle, the exact scope of which is left to be made explicit by the executive in one or more enabling decrees.—*Tr.*

ism with sympathy and enthusiasm. The Algerian people is quite aware of the fact that every blow struck against French oppression in Algeria dismantles the colonialist power.

Every ambush laid, every garrison blockaded and destroyed, every plane brought down sows panic among French colonial forces and strengthens the African or Madagascan or West Indian national consciousness.

The oppressed peoples know today that national liberation is a part of the process of historic development but they also know that this liberation must be the work of the oppressed people.

It is the colonial peoples who must liberate themselves from colonialist domination.

True liberation is not that pseudo-independence in which ministers having a limited responsibility hobnob with an economy dominated by the colonial pact.

Liberation is the total destruction of the colonial system, from the pre-eminence of the language of the oppressor and "departmentalization," to the customs union that in reality maintains the former colonized in the meshes of the culture, of the fashion, and of the images of the colonialist.

It is with tenacity and fervor that the Algerian people has undertaken this total destruction.

We do not expect this colonialism to commit suicide. It is altogether logical for it to defend itself fanatically. But it is, on the other hand, its awareness that it cannot survive which will determine its liquidation as a style of contact with other peoples.

The colonialist people will be cured of its racism and of its spiritual infirmity only if it shows a willingness to consider the former possession as an absolutely independent nation.

Any evocation of "former ties" or of unreal "communities" is a lie and a ruse.

The Algerian people has proved for nearly four years that this lie and this ruse are now being replaced by its truth and by its will.

8

A Continued Crisis

For the fourth time since November 1, 1954, France is without a government.

After the teams of Edgar Faure, Guy Mollet, Bourgès-Manoury, and the most recent one of Mr. Félix Gaillard which went by the name of a national union government, here we have a new crisis which all parties agree is an extremely grave one.

And surely no one today can fail to realize that the Algerian war is at the root of this governmental instability in France. Nevertheless it is necessary to try to grasp the internal development of the process responsible for this disequilibrium. The deterioration and disintegration of French prestige that these colonial wars have occasioned, within and outside of France, require clarification.

The analysis of the situation should enable us to gauge, to measure this internal fatality that is undermining France and that is leading it with an almost mechanical inevitability to multiplying crises, to confining itself in an atmosphere of crisis.

To say that the Algerian war is draining the finances and unbalancing the economy of France is of course to proclaim a truth. But it would be a mistake to regard this truth as in any way privileged. The facts of the matter were clearly brought out in the debates in the French National Assembly on the cost of operations in Algeria. While the international experts—in this case those who periodically refloat the French economy—calculated the cost at 800 billion francs, Mr. Lacoste claimed, with a

El Moudjahid, No. 23, May 5, 1958.

straight face, that the Algerian war was costing the country nothing.

The French parties of the Left, which are prisoners of a doctrinal oversimplification according to which the Right negotiates whenever it is asked to participate in the costs, have taken refuge in a resigned attitude and only await the day when the Right, finding its interests endangered, will abandon its chauvinism and vote in favor of as many colonial independences as anyone might wish.

We have on several occasions called attention to this mechanization of thinking and to the apparition of this fetishism of causes taken in the most automatic, the least dialectical sense.

This ideological weakness of a large proportion of the French political groupings sheds light on the conflict that has existed in the French body politic since November 1st, 1954. The Radical Party which has been pulverized since the historic congress of Lyon, the Socialist Party within which more and more heterogeneous trends appear, the MRP which has just revealed its contradictions by its recent refusal to back Mr. Bidault's proposed venture, even the French Communist Party, whose monolithic structure has not preserved it from divergencies and oppositions on the theme of the Algerian war, each of these parties, according to its own style, manifests the incoherence of its positions, the violence of its conflicts, in short a fundamental disagreement.

The European contradictions

It would, however, be the worst of mistakes to isolate this destruction of French political life from the European and international context.

The European nations, especially Italy, England, and West Germany, for reasons of economic competition in Europe or of outlets to be preserved in Africa, have felt the necessity of manifesting an implicit hostility to the colonial wars waged by France.

To take an example: the Italian people, which has for a long time remained silent in the face of the support given by its government to the French colonial war, alerted by the Italian democratic groupings, has for some months been bestirring itself and is demanding in an imperative way the non-commitment of the Italian government alongside of French colonialism.

In West Germany it is now established that not one German newspaper dares support French policy. The French representatives in Germany can verify several times a day that the German people as a whole condemns French colonialism and extends its sympathy to the glorious Algerian people.

In England, the conservatives, who for a long time felt an identity of interests with the French colonialists, some months ago began an about-face and their press no longer conceals their position on the necessity for negotiations with the Algerian people.

This change in direction of the Western democracies is the consequence on the one hand of an undeniable anticolonial and liberal current, but especially—there is no use mincing matters —of the desire to see France reduced to its sole European dimension, amputated of its colonies, deprived of the preferential arrangements introduced by the colonial pact, and having at last to meet the other European national economies on an equal, free, competitive level. Seen in this other light, the formula of "Africa, France's restricted hunting ground," tends to be replaced by a second formula, "Africa, Europe's restricted hunting ground."

Western contradictions and international pressures

The United States of America, face to face with the communist world, is developing an African policy which fundamentally corresponds to the new European positions. American democrats, when they set forth their position on the decolonization of Africa, always emphasize the necessity for the United States not to share the French colonialist outlook.

The prevailing theme of their argument is clear: in Africa

France is in the process of compromising the possibilities of the West and of the "white man."

Two other elements, however, qualify the progressive modification of the American attitude. And the first of these is the acute certainty, on the other side of the Atlantic, that the time has come to make a choice, to support the struggle for independence of the colonial peoples, to give a hand to the disintegration of empires, to support the liberation of the oppressed peoples. Moreover, in the face of the "communist danger," within the framework of the Cold War and the division of the world into spheres of influence, the United States is more and more aware of the urgency of positions radically opposed to French colonialism.

On an international level, it is worth emphasizing the immense enthusiasm aroused throughout the Afro-Asiatic countries by the epic struggle which the Algerian people has been waging for nearly four years.

From Bandung to Cairo to Accra, all the Afro-Asiatic peoples, all the oppressed of yesterday bear, support, and increasingly assume the cause of the Algerian Revolution; it is absolutely not exaggerated to say that, more and more, France will have two continents against her in Algeria.

It is through their failure to analyze these multiple factors, these dialectical contradictions, that the French political parties so often find themselves in a state of uncertainty, of passionate exacerbation without a guiding line, of anxiety—all of which suggests a self-destructive pattern of behavior.

The atmosphere of crisis

In France, the failure to establish a coherent political line on Algeria does not pertain to the political groups alone.

Within each party today a Center, a Right, and a Left can be distinguished. On the level of the popular masses or of special bodies like the Church, one is struck by a mood of uneasiness, of bitterness, and of despair. There is not one association, not one group of men or of women that is not affected by the development of the Algerian war: a split in the students' associations, a split in the teaching body, an upheaval in the army, a call to order of the cardinals, disaffection in the police. All these phenomena, by their number and their gravity, indicate the confusion that prevails in the moral and political life of France.

The Algerian people's will to liberation challenges the fiction of a French Algeria beyond any peradventure of doubt. But it is also a certain type of behavior, a style of intellectual contact, that is thoroughly discredited. The Algerian people's fight is a radical criticism of the pseudo-right of property (*our* Africa south of the Sahara, *our* Algeria) and at the same time a challenge to the French people to criticize itself, to rid itself of the colonialist, anti-democratic and racist mentality, in short to live and to go beyond the historically elaborated contradictions.

The struggle of the Algerian people, a source of truth

The confusion that prevails at present in French moral and political life would be incomprehensible if it were not dialectically related to international realities and to the struggle of the Algerian people.

The decisive and implacable criticisms of Senator [John F.] Kennedy, the fundamentally anti-colonialist positions adopted by the British Laborites and, more generally, the recent position adopted by the American official services, reveal two phenomena. In the first place, the historic and general process of liberation of colonial peoples is recognized, identified, and accepted; also the certainty has been acquired, after analysis, that the Algerian people has put its whole weight behind the struggle and that it is really hard to see how France could fail to recognize Algeria's independence.

Mr. Lacoste has not become unpopular in the world and in French public opinion because he has directed the repression or justified the collective murders, but because Mr. Lacoste's lie has appeared in full daylight, because he has been betrayed and unmasked by the invincibility of the Algerian National Army. The indefinitely protracted "last moments," the bulletins of total victory, the fanciful proclamations, the bluff, explain the confusion and the ambivalence that his name arouses. The Left condemns him because he is opposed to a Leftist policy, and the Right because he has not kept his promises, because he has not pacified Algeria, because the military situation is becoming more and more serious.

Thus a French political crisis exists, not because there are opposed political views or because there are divergent world views, but because the Algerian people's will to liberation constitutes a scandal which upsets the established balances, the accepted truths and fundamentally challenges the prospects of the French nation.

The French crisis does not develop in a closed circle. It is not a crisis of pure reflection. It is in the most tragic practice that the French people is rethinking and reconstructing its system of values.

In intensifying its military effort, the French people has imposed upon the Algerian people immense sacrifices, but it is precisely the dialectical development of this combat that was to produce in turn an ideological upheaval in France and make dazzlingly clear that the French effort went counter to history, to morality, to everything human.

It is the desperate, stubborn, heroic struggle of the Algerian people which makes apparent new meanings, overcomes certain contradictions, makes possible what yesterday was unthinkable.

Mr. Bidault's pre-investiture declarations did not dissatisfy and irritate because they were poorly composed. It is because Mr. Bidault clearly indicated that he had understood nothing, that he had not followed events, that he was disconnected from history, that he was outside of time. This new time, these new conditions, these original realities are being introduced precisely by the combat of the Algerian people.

It is the struggle of the Algerian people which has set into motion this transformation of French political life. It is through contact with this national will, with the violence with which its demands are put forth, that French political prospects are being remodeled.

These prospects are being conditioned by pressures from

three sources: European pressures—because after all, if Africa is lost for France this should not mean that it is lost for Europe—; international pressures—for the Communist hydra might very well settle in Africa if the combined West were to maintain the silence of an accessory in the face of France's bellicosity—; pressures of the Algerian people, the most active and also the truest element in this dialectic. These three orders of factors circumscribe the French national reality and induce, bring out, and unmask the essential contradictions of a colonialist and racist country having paradoxically democratic aspirations.

And it is not true that this confrontation can cease by magic. It is not true that the hand of America or of Italy can be forced. It is not true that Mr. Pineau can, if he should ask for it, get the support of NATO. It is not true that with a little good will Mr. Mendès-France can come to terms with Mr. Morice or that Mr. André Philip can fraternize with Mr. Mollet. It is not true that Mr. Bigeard's general staff can come up with something new in the Algerian war. All these impossibilities are the negatives of a major reality: France is plunged in an atmosphere of cataclysmic crisis and it will escape from it only by negotiation with the FLN.

9

Letter to the Youth of Africa

For four years the Algerian people has waged a very hard combat against French colonialism. You cannot fail to be aware of the colossal effort that France has made in Algeria to maintain its domination. And you know that the FLN which leads our struggle has always fiercely resisted the French war of reconquest.

We have already on several occasions addressed the colonial countries in general and it has always appeared to us important to point to certain failures and to the appearance of totally unexpected concepts.

For three years we have said repeatedly that the wedge driven into the French colonial system by the liberation of Indochina, of Tunisia, and of Morocco had shaken its infrastructure, but that there was no room for any illusions, and that the beast was still quite robust.

The colonial world has during the past fifteen years been subjected to increasingly violent assaults and the fractured edifice is in the process of crumbling. No one today challenges the fact that this liquidation of colonialism constitutes the specific mark of the postwar period. The historic process, resulting from the multiple contradictions inherent in the capitalist system and given dynamism by the national will of the oppressed peoples, presides over the birth of independent states.

The colonized peoples have generally recognized themselves in each of the movements, in each of the revolutions set into motion and carried through by the oppressed. Beyond the necessary solidarity with the men who, throughout the earth, are fighting for democracy and respect for their rights, there has been imposed, with unaccustomed violence, the firm decision of the colonized peoples to want for themselves and for their brothers the recognition of their national existence, of their existence as members of an independent, free, and sovereign State.

For many years the history of the world, the history of men's struggle for dignity, has confronted peoples with definite problems. Men enslaved and oppressed by foreign nations are invited today to participate totally in the work of demolition of the colonial system. And it is not an exaggeration to say that if those parts of the world where national existence has already been realized mark time without overcoming their contradictions, it is precisely because any new step toward progress implies the liberation of the colonies.

It is essential that the oppressed peoples join up with the peoples who are already sovereign if a humanism that can be considered valid is to be built to the dimensions of the universe.

For ten years the duty of every colonized being has been clear: it is, on the national soil, to undermine the colonialist edifice and support in a positive way the struggles of colonized peoples.

The war of liberation of the Algerian people has spread the gangrene and carried the rot of the system to such a point that it has become obvious to observers that a global crisis must result.

It is in anticipation of this possible mutation, of this possible general reckoning, that we have on many occasions addressed ourselves to your representatives in the French parliamentary assemblies and to your trade union leaders.

For three years we have repeatedly invited them to bring the colonialist beast to bay, to oblige it to release its clutch; for three years we have repeatedly explained to your representatives that they must combine their efforts and shatter the French empire, since the Algerian people for its part was waging on its territory an open, noble, and difficult war.

Truth requires that we tell you that nearly all your representatives, mystified by a very grave phenomenon of alienation, have always opposed to our approaches the respect for French republican legality.

Now it seems that we have at least three points in common. To begin with, our respective nations have been militarily occupied, economically exploited, and culturally mute, since the three-colored flag has been waving over them.

Every urge toward an expression of our nation that is in conformity with its history, faithful to its tradition, and linked to the very sap of its soil finds itself limited, stopped, broken.

The style of the colonial pact that governs the multi-dimensional exploitation of the territories of the "French Union" constitutes our second point in common. It is not enough to say that France occupies our national soil; it has had the nerve to install itself here and has not hesitated to draw up a whole legislation, an entire code in terms of which our national essence is denied for the benefit of the French order.

The will to independence that had to constitute the only response to this colonization is the third point that the peoples dominated by France have in common. When we address ourselves to the colonial peoples and more especially to the African peoples, it is both because we have to hurry to build Africa, so that it will express itself and come into being, so that it will enrich the world of men, and so that it may be authentically enriched by the world's contributions. It is also because the sole means of achieving this result is to break the back of the most frenzied, the most intractable, the most barbarous colonialism in existence.

At the present time all movements of liberation of colonial peoples, whichever the dominating nations may be, are linked to the existence of French colonialism.

"The French Empire," by its scope, still today enjoys a certain prestige and an apparent stability. The viciousness of French colonialism, its contempt for international morality, its

spectacular barbarousness, reassure the other colonialist countries.

You of the colonial countries!

You must know that the future of your national existence,
the cause of your freedom and of your independence are at stake
in Algeria at this very moment.

It is not true, as some of the colonial "parliamentarians" sitting in the French Assemblies have claimed, that the Algerian
war is promoting the process of decolonization and that conse-
quently it is sufficient to exploit these difficulties of French
colonialism on the parliamentary level.

It is true that the *Loi-Cadre* voted under the pressure of the
Algerian war has initiated a relaxation of the stranglehold on
the countries of Africa, but we believe it would be a grave
mistake to see this "evolution" as more than a caricature.

What the colonial countries want is not a "kind gesture" on
the part of the master, but quite literally the death of this master. Moreover, within the very framework of this evolution, it is
a common thing to be confronted with the "bad will" of the
French administrators, their impatience with the crumb of
freedom allowed the "Negroes," their fury at this affront to
white supremacy. And certain colonial parliamentarians do not
even fear to expose themselves to ridicule by threatening to
recall French administrators hostile to the *Loi-Cadre*.

A sound analysis of French colonialism in the fourth year of
the Algerian war should have led these parliamentarians to look
upon such "bad will" less as an individual fact than as the expression of a colonialism still holding very solidly to its position,
and as the sign that in France everything would be done to
prevent any kind of evolution of the colonial countries and any
attack on the colonial pact.

What is happening today in France, in Algeria, is inherently
part of the same process as the "bad will" of administrators or of
settlers.

Youth of the colonial countries!

For four years we have constantly repeated to those who sit in the French Assemblies that French colonialism will not yield to any magic operation and that it is futile to hope for its progressive disappearance.

The future will have no pity for those men who, possessing the exceptional privilege of being able to speak words of truth to their oppressors, have taken refuge in an attitude of passivity, of mute indifference, and sometimes of cold complicity.

Mr. Houphouët-Boigny, African deputy and President of the RDA,[1] granted an interview to the press a few days ago. After expressing some absurd views on the hoped-for evolution of an Africa draped in the three-colored flag, he came to the Algerian question and did not hesitate to say that Algeria must remain within the French orbit.

This gentleman, for more than three years, has played the role of straw-man for French colonialism. Holding a post in every government, Mr. Houphouët-Boigny has directly associated himself with the policy of extermination practiced in Algeria.

With Mr. Lacoste at his right and Messrs. Morice or Chaban-Delmas at his left, Mr. Houphouët-Boigny has endorsed, in a way that cannot be pardoned, a policy that has brought mourning to the Algerian nation and compromised the development of our country for many years.

Mr. Houphouët-Boigny has become the traveling salesman of French colonialism and he has not feared to appear before the United Nations to defend the French thesis.

Mr. Houphouët-Boigny is a doctor of medicine. He was Mr. Gaillard's Minister of Health. It was under his reign that the raid on Sakiet Sidi Youssef occurred. The ambulances of the International Red Cross were machine-gunned, bombarded, gutted. Scores of women and children were cut in two by the volleys of French aviation.

The African Houphouët-Boigny, the doctor of medicine Houphouët-Boigny, have, neither of them, feared to assume this

[1] RDA—*Rassemblement Démocratique Africain,* African Democratic Assembly.—*Tr.*

barbarism and to affirm their solidarity with the French military.

Mr. Houphouët-Boigny, like a good minister of the French Republic, considered it his duty to approve of Sakiet, to congratulate the valiant French army, and to support the pressures on the Tunisian government with full ministerial solidarity.

In the fine hours of French imperialism, it could be a kind of honor for a colonized person to be a part of the French government. This honor without responsibility or risk, this childish complacency about being a minister or Secretary of State, could, in an extreme case, be forgiven.

In the past ten years, however, it has become truly intolerable and unacceptable for Africans to hold a post in the government that dominates them.

Every colonized person who today accepts a governmental post must know clearly that he will sooner or later be called upon to sponsor a policy of repression, of massacres, of collective murders in one of the regions of "the French Empire."

When a colonized person like Mr. Houphouët-Boigny is so forgetful of the racism of the settlers, of the wretchedness of his people, of the shameless exploitation of his country that he does not participate in the liberating pulsation that lifts up the oppressed peoples, and allows the Bigeards, the Massus, and their ilk to be given full powers, we must not hesitate to state that this is a case of treason, of complicity, and of incitation to murder.

Youth of Africa, of Madagascar, of the West Indies, the soldiers of your respective countries drafted by force into the French army have enthusiastically rallied to the ranks of the National Liberation Army. Today, side by side with the Algerian patriots, they carry on a heroic struggle against the common enemy.

The FLN which leads the combat of the Algerian people addresses you and asks you to exert pressure on your deputies to oblige them to desert the French Assemblies.

The time has come for all colonials to participate in the routing of the French colonialists.

Wherever you may be, you must know that the moment has come for all of us to unite our efforts and deal the death blow to French imperialism.

Youth of Africa! Youth of Madagascar! Youth of the West Indies! We must, all of us together, dig the grave in which colonialism will finally be entombed!

10

First Truths on the Colonial Problem

The twentieth century, when the future looks back on it, will not only be remembered as the era of atomic discoveries and interplanetary explorations. The second upheaval of this period, unquestionably, is the conquest by the peoples of the lands that belong to them.

Jostled by the claims for national independence by immense regions, the colonialists have had to loosen their stranglehold. Nevertheless, this phenomenon of liberation, of triumph of national independence, of retreat of colonialism, does not manifest itself in a unique manner. Every former colony has a particular way of achieving independence. Every new sovereign state finds itself practically under the obligation of maintaining definite and preferential relations with the former oppressor.

The parties that lead the struggle against colonialist oppression, at a certain phase of the combat, decide for practical reasons to accept a fragment of independence with the firm intention of arousing the people again within the framework of the fundamental strategy of the total evacuation of the territory and of the effective seizure of all national resources. This style, which has taken form on a succession of occasions, is today well known. On the other hand, there is a whole opposite dialectic which, it seems, has not received sufficient attention.

A first condition:
"The Rights" of the former occupant

Some decades ago, the colonialist rulers could indefinitely propound the highly civilizing intentions of their countries. The

El Moudjahid, No. 27, July 22, 1958.

concessions, the expropriations, the exploitation of the workers, the great wretchedness of the peoples, were traditionally conjured away and denied. Afterwards, when the time came to withdraw from the territory, the colonialists were forced to discard their masks. In the negotiations on independence, the first matters at issue were the economic interests: banks, monetary areas, research permits, commercial concessions, inviolability of properties stolen from the peasants at the time of the conquest, etc. . . . Of civilizing, religious, or cultural works, there was no longer any question. The time had come for serious things, and trivialities had to be left behind. Such attitudes were to open the eyes of men struggling in other regions of the world.

The actual rights of the occupant were then perfectly identified. The minority that came from the mother country, the university missions, technical assistance, the friendship affirmed and reaffirmed, were all relegated to a secondary level. The important thing was obviously the real rights that the occupant meant to wrench from the people, as the price for a piece of independence.

The acceptance of a nominal sovereignty and the absolute refusal of real independence—such is the typical reaction of colonialist nations with respect to their former colonies. Neo-colonialism is impregnated with a few ideas which both constitute its force and at the same time prepare its necessary decline.

In the course of the struggle for liberation, things are not clear in the consciousness of the fighting people. Since it is a refusal, at one and the same time, of political non-existence, of wretchedness, of illiteracy, of the inferiority complex so subtly instilled by oppression, its battle is for a long time undifferentiated. Neo-colonialism takes advantage of this indetermination. Armed with a revolutionary and spectacular good will, it grants the former colony everything. But in so doing, it wrings from it an economic dependence which becomes an aid and assistance program.

We have seen that this operation usually triumphs. The

novelty of this phase is that it is necessarily brief. This is because it takes the people little time to realize that nothing fundamental has changed. Once the hours of effusion and enthusiasm before the spectacle of the national flag floating in the wind are past, the people rediscovers the first dimension of its requirement: bread, clothing, shelter.

Neo-colonialism, because it proposes to do justice to human dignity in general, addresses itself essentially to the middle class and to the intellectals of the colonial country.

Today, the peoples no longer feel their bellies at peace when the colonial country has recognized the value of its elites. The people want things really to change and right away. Thus it is that the struggle resumes with renewed violence.

In this second phase, the occupant bristles and unleashes all his forces. What was wrested by bombardments is reconverted into results of free negotiations. The former occupant intervenes, in the name of duty, and once again establishes his war in an independent country.

All the former colonies, from Indonesia to Egypt, without forgetting Panama, which have tried to denounce the agreements wrung from them by force, have found themselves obliged to undergo a new war and sometimes to see their sovereignty again violated and amputated.

The notorious "rights" of the occupant, the false appeal to a common past, the persistence of a rejuvenated colonial pact, are the permanent bases of an attack directed against national sovereignty.

A second obstacle: the zones of influence

The concern to maintain the former colony in the yoke of economic oppresssion is obviously not sadism. It is not out of wickedness or ill-will that such an attitude is adopted. It is because the handling of their national riches by the colonized peoples compromises the economic equilibrium of the former occupant. The reconversion of the colonial economy, the industries engaged in processing raw materials from the underdevel-

oped territories, the disappearance of the colonial pact, competition with foreign capital, constitute a mortal danger for imperialism.

For countries like Great Britain and France there arises the
important question of zones of influence. Unanimous in their
decision to stifle the national aspirations of the colonial peoples,
these countries wage a gigantic struggle for the seizure of world
markets. The economic battles between France, England, and
the United States, in the Middle East, in the Far East, and now
in Africa, give the measure of imperialist voracity and bestiality.
And it is not an exaggeration to say that these battles are the
direct cause of the strategies which, still today, shake the newly
independent states. In exceptional circumstances, the zones of
influence of the pound sterling, of the dollar, and of the franc,
are converted and become, by a conjurer's trick, the Western
world. Today in Lebanon and in Iraq, if we are to believe Mr.
Malraux, it is *homo occidentalis* who is threatened.

The oil of Iraq has removed all prohibitions and made concrete the true problems. We have only to remember the violent
interventions in the West Indian archipelago or in Latin America every time the dictatorships supported by American policy
were in danger. The Marines who today are being landed in
Beirut are the brothers of those who, periodically, are sent to
reestablish "order" in Haiti, in Costa Rica, in Panama. The
United States considers that the two Americas constitute a
world governed by the Monroe Doctrine whose application is
entrusted to the American forces. The single article of this doctrine stipulates that America belongs to the Americans, in other
words, to the State Department.

Its outlets having proved insufficient, it was inevitable that
America would turn to other regions, namely the Far East, the
Middle East, and Africa. There ensued a competition between
beasts of prey; its creations are: the Eisenhower doctrine against
England in the Middle East; support for Ngo Dinh Diem
against France in Indochina; Economic Aid Commisson in Af-

rica announced by the presidential voyage of Mr. Nixon, against France, England, and Belgium.

Every struggle for national liberation must take zones of influence into account.

The cold war

This competitive strategy of Western nations, moreover, enters into the vaster framework of the policy of the two blocs, which for ten years has held a definite menace of atomic disintegration suspended over the world. And it is surely not purely by chance that the hand or the eye of Moscow is discovered, in an almost stereotyped way, behind each demand for national independence, put forth by a colonial people. This is because any difficulty that is put in the way of the supremacy of the West in any given section of the world is a concrete threat to its economic power, to the range of its military strategic bases, and represents a limiting of its potential.

Every challenge to the rights of the West over a colonial country is experienced both as a weakening of the Western world and as a strengthening of the Communist world.

Today an island like Cyprus, which has almost no resources of its own and which has a population of barely half a million people, is the object of violent rivalries. And even NATO, an organization designed to parry a Soviet invasion, is being endangered by the problem to which the isle of Cyprus gives rise.

The third bloc

The position taken by a few newly independent countries, which are determined to remain outside the policy of the coalitions, has introduced a new dimension into the balance of forces in the world. Adopting the so-called policy of positive neutralism, of non-dependence, of non-commitment, of the third force, the underdeveloped countries that are awakening from a long slumber of slavery and of oppression, have considered it their duty to remain outside of any warlike involvement, in order to devote themselves to the urgent economic tasks, to staving off hunger, to the improvement of man's lot.

And what the West has in truth not understood is that today a new humanism, a new theory of man is coming into being, which has its root in man. It is easy to regard President Nehru as indecisive because he refuses to harness himself to Western imperialism, and Presidents Nasser or Sukarno as violent when they nationalize their companies or demand the fragments of their territories that are still under foreign domination. What no one sees is that the 350 million Hindus, who have known the hunger of British imperialism, are now demanding bread, peace, and well-being. The fact is that the Egyptian *fellahs* and the Indonesian *boys,* whom Western writers like to feature in their exotic novels, insist on taking their own destiny into their hands and refuse to play the role of an inert panorama that had been reserved for them.

The prestige of the West

And we here touch upon a psychological problem which is perhaps not fundamental but which enters into the framework of the dialectics that is now developing. The West, whose economic system is the standard (and by virtue of that fact oppressive), also prides itself on its humanist superiority. The Western "model" is being attacked in its essence and in its finality. The Orientals, the Arabs, and the Negroes, today, want to present their plans, want to affirm their values, want to define their relations with the world. The negation of political *beni-oui-ouism*[1] is linked to the refusal of economic *beni-oui-ouism* and of cultural *beni-oui-ouism*. It is no longer true that the promotion of values passes through the screen of the West. It is not true that we must constantly trail behind, follow, depend on someone or other. All the colonial countries that are waging the struggle today must know that the political independence that they will wring from the enemy in exchange for the maintenance of an economic dependency is only a snare and a delu-

[1] *beni-oui-oui,* a yes-man.

sion, that the second phase of total liberation is necessary because required by the popular masses, that this second phase, because it is a capital one, is bound to be hard and waged with iron determination, that, finally, at that stage, it will be necessary to take the world strategy of coalition into account, for the West simultaneously faces a double problem: the communist danger and the coming into being of a third neutral coalition, represented essentially by the underdeveloped countries.

The future of every man today has a relation of close dependency on the rest of the universe. That is why the colonial peoples must redouble their vigilance and their vigor. A new humanism can be achieved only at this price. The wolves must no longer find isolated lambs to prey upon. Imperialism must be blocked in all its attempts to strengthen itself. The peoples demand this; the historic process requires it.

11

The Lesson of Cotonou

The Congress adopts the slogan of immediate independence and decides to take all necessary measures to mobilize the African masses round this slogan and to translate this will to independence into reality.

These are the words that conclude the declaration of war that has just been addressed, from Cotonou, to the French Government of General de Gaulle by the peoples of Africa south of the Sahara.

Already in September, 1957, in Bamako, the security apparatus set up by the *Loi-Cadre* had collapsed. The traitor Houphouët-Boigny and his accomplices had had to draw back before the African demand for national independence. All the specialists in colonial lethargy had then betaken themselves to the spot in order to see their victory consecrated.

In Bamako, however, the Africans rejected the *Loi-Cadre,* rejected the irresponsibility to which colonialism condemned them.

In Bamako the safety lock in Africa south of the Sahara was smashed. A process was set into motion. Cotonou is the preliminary of the great struggle for liberation as a result of which more than 30 million Africans will achieve independence.

One remembers the euphoria that prevailed in French political circles after the *Loi-Cadre* was voted. For once, it was claimed, France takes the initiative and, in accordance with "its most essential tradition," anticipates the peoples' aspiration. As it happens, the lucid observer of things concerning Africa south of the Sahara knew perfectly well that the Defferre law was infinitely short of the aspirations of the African masses.

The African workers, the African students, have for several years been held in leash by the African parliamentarians.

Since 1947 French colonialism has owed its tranquility to the unqualifiable treason of certain African elites.

Since 1947 in a very diffuse way, and in a much more concerted way since 1953, African trade unionists have been developing their action in accordance with a deliberately national outlook.

At a far remove from any craft-union tendency, aimed on the one hand at the Africanization of the leaders, and on the other at nationalization, hence at independence, the action of the trade unions has imparted an absolutely new style to the struggle against French colonialism.

The UGTAN,[1] which extends its network over the entire country, is gradually asphyxiating the colonialist beast. In the face of the workers who demand the nationalization and the socialization of enterprises and of properties, colonialism at bay is preparing to mobilize new mercenaries to defend Western civilization in Africa south of the Sahara.

The Federation of Students of Africa south of the Sahara, for its part, has for several years been carrying on a work of propaganda in depth, a campaign of demystification, of putting forward clear slogans. This is why the police of the traitor Houphouët-Boigny have persecuted, arrested, and tortured students from Africa south of the Sahara.

The cancellation of scholarships, the seizure and prohibition of the Student Federation's paper—these are operations carried on under the authority of Houphouët-Boigny. Moreover, in Africa south of the Sahara, the students who are opposed to the policy of treason of certain leaders of the RDA [*Rassemblement Démocratique Africain*] are not employed as civil servants by the ridiculous government councils; they are shifted, dismissed, expelled from the territory. Despite these police maneuvers,

---

[1] UGTAN—*Union Générale des Travailleurs d'Afrique Noire*, General Union of the Workers of Black Africa.—*Tr.*

despite these measures of intimidation, the students of Africa south of the Sahara, in Cotonou, through their president, have affirmed their decision to go over to direct action and to wrest their national independence by force of arms.

Mr. Defferre, who was to attach his name to this parody of liberal policy, has since had time to meditate on "the ingratitude of the Africans." With the *Loi-Cadre,* French colonialism hoped to have contracted a guarantee of a good twenty years against the nationalist virus. The *Loi-Cadre* made official the division of the African continent, scattered government councils here and there, set up competitive economic areas. Centralization, territorial unity, the constitution of the nation, the economic integration of the country, was replaced by the hideous Balkanization of Africa south of the Sahara.

Mr. Houphouët-Boigny's mistake, and that of his accomplices, was to have taken insufficient account of the Algerian battering ram which for four years has been shaking the French empire to its foundations.

For having clung to Algeria beyond the point of common sense, French colonialism has doomed itself to extinction. With the end of the war in Algeria, with the victory of the armed forces of the ALN and the independence of Algeria, the whole French imperial system will collapse.

The resolution of the Cotonou Congress is important not only because it establishes immediate independence as its objective. The very terms in which this independence is demanded, the social content, the clarity with which the notions of socialism, of collectivization, of progressive community are used, indicate that the Africans are not aiming at a purely formal independence.

In Cotonou what we have witnessed is not an evolution of African minds, but an essential change which leads to the effective taking over of the country by the people.

Since Cotonou, French colonialism has been paralyzed and made voiceless.

Now it so happens that, because the Algerian Revolution

exists in Africa, the claim to nationality of the other African peoples finds broad inspiration in the very movement of our Revolution. For four years, the very existence of colonialism in Africa has been shattered to pieces by the Algerian people and it is a commonplace to recognize today that a certain number of countries which are independent in 1958 would surely not have been so if French colonialism, among others, had not had to face the innumerable blows that the Algerian people has dealt it.

Guy Mollet, Bourgès-Manoury, Gaillard, Pflimlin, de Gaulle "the savior of France"—pre-fascist before becoming totally so— are the various historic accidents that have been provoked in France by the armed encounter of the national will of the Algerian people and of the will to colonialist oppression of the French governments.

This curve of French political life evolving, since 1954, from Social Democracy unfaithful to its most elementary principles, to fascist and military dictatorship, is the very negation of the revolutionary heroism of the Algerian people.

This is why, henceforth, there can be no hesitation in Africa on the part of the national masses. Immediately and with a violent bracing of their shoulders, they find themselves equal to an immediate and total demand for national independence.

French colonialism seeks a colonialist response to the African national aspirations expressed in Cotonou. Certain observers think that de Gaulle will find a half-way measure between the *Loi-Cadre* and independence.

The FLN, after an analysis of the facts and in the light of the insurmountable difficulties that it creates for France in Algeria, is of the view that the peoples of Africa south of the Sahara under French domination must not withdraw but on the contrary, show with firmness and uncompromisingly, that the time for confused solutions is irrevocably past.

France has been pushed back on her heels; she must be pushed back further. We must cut off all her avenues of escape, asphyxiate her without pity, kill in her every attempt at domination. In 1958, France is incapable, materially and humanly, economically and politically incapable of undertaking a war in Africa south of the Sahara.

That is why the African people must go forward, increase their pressure and demand, right now, their independence. The African masses and the African elites must make arrangements at once to pass over to direct action, take arms, sow panic in the colonialist ranks.

The FLN and the ALN are ready, for their part, to help the African peoples in their struggle for liberation. It shall not be said that French imperialism after its departure from Algeria can still maintain itself in Africa. The slogan today must be:

"Africans, men and women of Africa, to arms! Death to French colonialism!"

12

Appeal to Africans

When, under the pressure of the African masses, General de Gaulle in the course of his voyage overseas had to define the meaning of the referendum—for the territories under colonial domination—the French Left and international opinion thought they could see in this statement the first manifestation of what people like to call the liberalism of the head of the French government.

After the first hours of surprise it was of course necessary to refer back to the texts, to the realities, and therefore to the concrete possibilities left to the men of Africa south of the Sahara.

In reality, thanks to the referendum operation, General de Gaulle is involving all the "French possessions" in an indefinite process of freely consented domestication. To begin with, what does the referendum mean, when considered in the light of African national aspirations? French colonialism relinquishes its reliance on its army, and its police, on its traditional *beni-oui-ouis,* and looks for its support to local assemblies which have been abundantly compromised and devaluated.

While in certain states the Government Council has taken the position of demanding national independence, French colonialism in the majority of cases has been able to rely on the support of African politicians.

The Africans who ask their compatriots to vote for de Gaulle and "the Franco-African Community" by plebiscite, show a profound lack of understanding of the problems of decolonization and a criminal ignorance of the national aspirations of the African peoples.

El Moudjahid, No. 29, September 17, 1958.

Participation in the vote, casting a ballot on questions that are strictly French, gives substance to that "French Union" necessarily transformed into a "Franco-African Community," alienates the African personality and, as the constitution says, establishes a single nationality.

Participating in the vote means tacitly recognizing oneself as a member of the same family, of the same nation having common problems, whereas in reality each African who votes in the referendum will bind his people and his country a little more closely to French colonialism.

The massive presence of French military and police forces in Africa south of the Sahara, the agitation of the compromised politicians, their statements, their urgent invitations to their people to vote yes, the traditions of gerrymandering, leave no doubt as to the results of the referendum in Africa south of the Sahara.

In a certain number of states, the French constitution will be adopted in the plebiscite vote by a very great majority.

Now it must be realized that by October 1st, four real problems will face the French and the Africans. Will the African states delegate deputies to the French National Assembly? Will the representation of 30 million Africans be proportional? Will the Africans have a right to discuss their budget, will they have the possibility of determining the investments concerning their respective territories? Does France intend, despite the opposition of the Africans, to bring about that "Eurafrica" which is to consecrate the break-up of Africa into European areas of influence and for the sole benefit of these European economies? Does France intend to maintain the African states in the framework of NATO? The African states, in the Bandung era, want to exist on an international level and demand their place in the UN. How does France hope to reconcile the maintenance of the colonial pact and the national existence of the African states?

All these questions will come up after the referendum, when African men and women come to measure the depth of the mystification.

Once again, French colonialism in the long run is playing a losing game. De Gaulle, in Africa, will have made no decisive contribution. The same problems will subsist, the same needs, the same demand for national independence.

French colonialism will oppose these demands with the same lack of good faith, the same methods. The struggle will therefore continue, though with the difference that the parliamentary phase seems to have been definitely discarded and that in Africa south of the Sahara the armed struggle for the liberation of the national territory is becoming increasingly imperative.

Once again French colonialism is shutting all the doors. Instead of inviting the authentic representatives of the peoples that it dominates to a constructive discussion that will lead to the end of the colonial pact and the recognition of individual national sovereignties, it perpetuates the cycle of lies, of terror, of war, thereby rendering the reconciliation of peoples extremely difficult.

13

Sequels of a Plebiscite in Africa

The success of a plebiscite, in obedience to a long-established pattern, ensures the authorities responsible for the *coup d'état* a longer or shorter period of enjoyment of power. The exercise of authority made possible by the plebiscite, if it is to be effective and reward the authors of the *putsch*, must enable them to derive the maximum of advantage over a maximum of time and in relative tranquility.

The combined action of the French colonialists, of the fascists with their pretorian vanguard in Algiers, and of the reactionary forces in France, has succeeded in imposing General de Gaulle's arbitration.

The preparation of the plot

The fascist forces of this plot were proposing to use the name of General de Gaulle to set up organizations capable of taking over effective power. These organizations would then get rid of the General-President.

During these past three months, in France and Algeria particularly, we have witnessed, round the kernel of the sedition-mongers of May 13th, a crystallization of all the racist, ultra-chauvinistic, fascist currents that exist among the French. We have witnessed similarly the colonization of the apparatus of the state by the members of these militias.

The measures, equally stereotyped, which always succeed a plebiscite were hastily announced: the bringing to their senses of those favoring the abandonment of Algeria and especially the outlawing of the opposition groups.

El Moudjahid, No. 30, October 10, 1958.

The colonialist forces, which have backed with their authority and totally supported the fascist undertaking, were haunted by the terror of any kind of process of decolonization. After the experiences of Tunisia and of Morocco, and the much more traumatizing one of Indochina, the colonialist circles had sworn to tolerate no more abandonments. And so these colonialist circles enthusiastically joined the fascist ranks to the cries of: *"Algérie française," "Halte à l'abandon!"*

At the same time the "empire hucksters" like Mendès-France and Edgar Faure found themselves accused of treason.

The colonialist circles have rallied to General de Gaulle because they considered him capable of keeping Algeria for France, of maintaining the French empire intact and perhaps, if the opportunity offered, of reconquering the lost territories.

The reactionaries who have responded to the fascist call were moved, for their part, mainly by the possibility afforded them of having, at no cost to themselves, forces paid for by the state whose interests were parallel to theirs to consolidate their authority in France and smash the action and the hopes of the French working class.

The victory

On the morrow of September 28th, the perpetrators of the *coup d'état* could therefore consider themselves satisfied. In the "Overseas" territories 98 percent of the colonials had answered "Yes" to General de Gaulle and to France. On French territory, 80 percent of the nationals having understood their interests and having detached themselves from subservience to the "alien parties" has approved in a mass the charter proposed by de Gaulle.

One week after the referendum, one week after that colossal, massive, miraculous success, the fascist enterprise began to vacillate. The Algerian war, around which the referendum was organized, the exploitation of which made possible the grandiose success pointed out by the press, limits the value of this plebiscite by its existence, its character, and its duration. On the morrow of September 28th, embarrassed by their 98 percent of votes, General de Gaulle and his henchmen no longer know where to turn. The reason for this is that new facts are daily being brought to light that qualify the significance of the "yeses."

... and the discomfiture

In West Africa, Mr. Mokhtar Ould Daddah, the Prime Minister of Mauritania, a territory which voted "yes" by 93 percent, declared on October 1st:

"I believe that the present territorial assembly should resign, to make possible the election in January of a new Assembly to which the present Government Council will offer its resignation. The new government and the new Assembly would choose the status member of State of the Community and would draw up the local constitution which will be submitted to the Mauritanian people by referendum." And Mr. Ould Daddah added: "We shall then, when the time comes, leave the community of free peoples, defined under Title 12, without on this account breaking our ties with France and the States of the Community, and we shall conclude with her the association agreements as defined under Title 13."

In Dahomey, where the percentage of votes is close to 98 percent, Mr. Apithy, president of the government Council, has just announced the necessity for the political leaders of Africa south of the Sahara to consult one another in order to adopt a common attitude in respect to France. Defining what he considers to be the meaning of Dahomey's "yes" vote, Mr. Apithy added: "Through the free choice of its masses and the free will of its elected representatives, the Dahoman State tomorrow will be born within the community. Fully autonomous, in peace and in the friendship maintained with the other African peoples as well as with the metropolis, this State could prepare its accession to the economic and social development that will enable it some day to become an independent associated State."

In Senegal, where the rallying to the "yeses" was by 97

percent, the trade union opposition and the youth groupings continue to exert pressure on Messrs. Senghor and Lamine Gueye. Already in Cotonou Mr. Senghor, who seems not to want to free himself from the confusion that reigns in his mind, had been obliged to support the independence of Africa south of the Sahara. By effecting a tactical alliance with his adversary, Lamine Gueye, he was able to deceive the African masses and make them vote "yes." But after the success of the plebiscite Senghor finds himself pushed into giving a specific meaning to Senegal's vote. It is a "yes"—he says—to African independence in the rediscovered unity.

It is obvious that Senghor will again attempt to hoodwink the Senegalese masses, but his possibilities of action are becoming progressively reduced. The recent statement by Mamadou Dia, president of the government Council of Senegal, is significant: "Our essential concern," he said, "is to prepare our independence."

In Niger, the government succeeded in blocking the nationalist policy of Djibo Bakary. It is to be noted that Niger comes second after Guinea, among African territories, in the number of negative votes cast. With the help of the colonialists and the administrators, the government was able to ensure the success of the electoral voting of September 28th, but it is clear that the Nigerian masses in the weeks to come are going to exert decisive action to demand that their claims for national independence be taken into consideration. Quite obviously, the least that the other territories of West Africa, including the faithful Ivory Coast, can do is to choose the status of autonomous State associated with France.

Mr. Houphouët-Boigny will perhaps attempt to defend his theory of integral federalism, but it is doubtful that he will succeed. West Africa, despite de Gaulle, despite the 13th of May, despite the referendum, will become federated into autonomous States, so that, at a later stage, it will be able to study with the French representatives ways and means of cooperation with the former metropolis.

In Equatorial Africa, things are much clearer. In the Gabon, colonialist circles have been shaken by the number of "noes": several tens of thousands.

The political force of the opposition in the Gabon is such that Mr. Léon M'Ba, the prime minister, on leaving Libreville on October 3rd in order to engage in discussions in Paris with the French government, announced his decision to create a State of the Gabon. But what is much more important is the announcement, a few days ago, of the setting up of a mission of the grand council of Equatorial Africa, which has been given the task of creating a single State in Central Africa. Mr. Rivierez, President of the Territorial Assembly of Oubangui-Chari, has begun consultations with the representatives of the Chad, the Middle Congo, and the Gabon in order to set up the State with its nationality and to prepare relations among the other territories of Africa and of France. The old *Loi-Cadre* which was meant to break Africa up into fragments is relegated to the museum of history, along with the other attempts made by colonialism to maintain itself.

In Madagascar, where the *beni-oui-ouist* Tsiranana had no compunction about interpreting the Madagascan "yes" as a "no" to Moscow, colonialism is in no better pass. Mr. Tsiranana, who is the Sid-Cara of Madagascar, in a statement made immediately after the referendum, admits that the Madagascans will at last see the realization of the Madagascan Republic.

In the West Indies there were people who expressed surprise at the percentage of "yeses" obtained because of the position taken by Mr. Aimé Césaire. Is the independence of the French West Indies possible today? Such is the question that Césaire had to face. He could reply in the affirmative, choose the independence of the West Indies and seek admission to the Caribbean federation. Did he consider that this federation that is coming into being was not sufficiently structured and still depended too narrowly on the British crown? What is certain is that in the West Indies as elsewhere no leader can have any illusions as to the value of his person or the love that the masses would bear him when the will to national independence of their country is involved.

The case of Guinea

In order to initiate the liberation of Africa south of the Sahara, one thing was necessary: one territory at least had to say "no" to General de Gaulle's Constitution. Guinea behind Mr. Sekou Touré entered upon independence.

The existence of an independent Guinea deeply and irreversibly unbalances the French colonial regime in Africa south of the Sahara. Having common frontiers with Senegal, Sudan, and the Ivory Coast, Guinea is going to crystallize round herself all the nationalist potentialities existing in Africa south of the Sahara. It has been claimed that the other African political leaders had rejected the "no" through fear of economic reprisals by the French government. No one, however, can fail to recognize the fragility of such arguments. Politicians like Houphouët-Boigny and the abbé Fulbert Youlou who have militated in favor of the "yeses" are in reality counter-revolutionaries, enemies of the national independence of Africa.

Today the Guinean Republic, recognized by an increasing number of nations, supported by the African patriots of all the territories, strengthens its authority and brushes aside all misgivings and all fears. The other leaders of Africa south of the Sahara, the same ones who predicted catastrophes for Guinea, are getting together and are discovering that the yoke of colonialism in Africa south of the Sahara broke a long time ago. The compulsory contact with the settler alone, the violence with which French domination was experienced, crumble away. The Soviet Union has just recognized the Guinean Republic and the African States, at the request of Tunisia, have just proposed to Mr. Sekou Touré the sending of a mission to study the concrete and technical needs of the young Republic.

To illustrate this African solidarity forged in the struggle against colonialism, the Provisional Government of the Guinean Republic is giving concrete form to the guiding lines that inspire our action and is analyzing the bonds of close collaboration that must exist between the new independent states of Africa.

Because independent Guinea exists, the men of Africa south of the Sahara will very soon be able to compare their fate with that of their brothers of yesterday, enslaved by French colonialism.

Mr. Houphouët-Boigny went to endless pains to convince the African peoples that the status of a native was the most enviable one. That without the protection of the French mother country, the Negroes of Africa south of the Sahara would be abandoned.

From Guinea, the bridgehead of liberty, will come the waves which will destroy French domination in Africa south of the Sahara.

The referendum in France

Foreign observers have generally been impressed by the percentage of positive votes obtained by General de Gaulle. The most optimistic forecasts were 65 to 70 percent. But it was by 80 percent that the referendum was adopted in France. A quick diagnosis was made according to which the French had manifested a disaffection for the political parties of the Left.

An analysis of the voting, however, suggests other conclusions. As against 17,600,000 "yeses" there are 4,600,000 "noes." A difference of thirteen million votes thus gives the measure of the President's prestige. The Communists show a very marked loss of strength, estimated at one third. Moreover, the political leaders of the Left, Badiou, Mendès-France, Bourgès-Manoury, who campaigned for the rejection of the Constitution, are considered the great losers in this electoral battle. It therefore seems that the referendum can be looked upon as having put the democratic prospects in France into cold storage.

The statements of political men like Mr. Defferre, however, introduce a dissonant note into the harmony of these results. Millions of French men and women voted "yes" in order that the Algerian war might come to an end. Others did so in order that the empire might remain intact. It has been seen that the referendum in the colonial territories was an irreversible first step in the direction of the liberation of the oppressed peoples, and General de Gaulle's last statement in Constantine is an authentic relaunching of the war. After having promised the "rebels" to let bygones be bygones, the president of the French Council, in the good old tradition of his colleagues of the defunct Fourth Republic, announces social and economic progress.

Having seized power in order to make peace in Algeria, de Gaulle provokes the extension of the conflict in France. Since August 24th, the French economic and strategic bases have been sabotaged by the action groups of the FLN. With war in Algeria and war in France, colonialism, its expeditionary corps, and its support bases are feeling the blows of the Algerian Revolution. Peace in Algeria, peace in France today, depend on the recognition by France of the independence of Algeria.

De Gaulle held in check by the Algerian people

One may legitimately wonder what are the causes of this deterioration of the situation in Africa south of the Sahara. How can so colossal a success as that obtained in the referendum turn so rapidly into discomfiture and defeat for colonialism?

If one does not constantly refer to the struggle of the Algerian people one runs the risk of not exactly understanding the evolution of the relations between the colonies and French domination.

Because they have proved themselves incapable of defeating the Algerian national army, the colonialist forces have found themselves shorn of all prestige, and the fear that they inspired in the colonized peoples has definitely disappeared. The war that the Algerian people has been waging for four years has paved the way for the French collapse in Africa. Henceforth the road is free for all the countries occupied by French colonialism.

The Algerian people, faithful to its pledge to extirpate every trace of French domination in Africa, carries on the battle.

General de Gaulle before November 1st will find himself obliged to recognize the autonomous states in Africa south of the Sahara. At the same time he promises civil service posts to Algerians.

The political poverty, the logical paradox, continues. But it is the sign of confusion, of historic blindness, hence of defeat.

14

The Algerian War and Man's Liberation

Frequently the analysis and appraisal of a given event prove inadequate and the conclusions paradoxical, precisely because the organic links between the particular event and the historic development of the surrounding whole have not been sufficiently taken into account.

Thus, to take an example, the dialectical strengthening that occurs between the movement of liberation of the colonized peoples and the emancipatory struggle of the exploited working classes of the imperialist countries is sometimes neglected, and indeed forgotten.

The worker and the colonized . . .

The process of liberation of man, independently of the concrete situations in which he finds himself, includes and concerns the whole of humanity. The fight for national dignity gives its true meaning to the struggle for bread and social dignity. This internal relation is one of the roots of the immense solidarity that unites the oppressed peoples to the exploited masses of the colonialist countries.

In the course of the different wars of national liberation that have succeeded one another during these past twenty years it was not rare to note a suggestion of hostility, indeed of hate, in the attitude of the colonialist worker toward the colonized. This can be explained by the fact that the retreat of imperialism and the reconversion of the underdeveloped structures specific to the colonial state are immediately accompanied by economic crises that the workers in the colonialist country are the first to feel. The "metropolitan" capitalists allow social advantages and wage increases to be wrung from them by their workers to the exact extent to which the colonialist state allows them to exploit and make raids on the occupied territories. At the critical point at which the colonized peoples fling themselves into the struggle and demand their independence a critical period elapses in the course of which, paradoxically, the interest of the "metropolitan" workers and peasants seems to go counter to that of the colonized peoples. The damage caused by this "unexpected" alienation must be recognized and energetically counteracted.

The struggle against colonialism, in its specific aspect of exploitation of man by man, thus belongs in the general process of man's liberation. If the solidarity between "metropolitan" workers and colonized peoples can undergo crises and tensions, it is rare to find these among colonized peoples. The colonized have this in common, that their right to constitute a people is challenged. To diversify and legitimize this general attitude of the colonialist we find racism, hatred, contempt on the part of the oppressor, and correlatively stultification, illiteracy, moral asphyxiation, and endemic undernourishment in the oppressed.

Solidarity of the colonized.

Among colonized peoples there seems to exist a kind of illuminating and sacred communication as a result of which each liberated territory is for a certain time promoted to the rank of "guide territory." The independence of a new territory, the liberation of the new peoples are felt by the other oppressed countries as an invitation, an encouragement, and a promise. Every setback of colonial domination in America or in Asia strengthens the national will of the African peoples. It is in the national struggle against the oppressor that colonized peoples have discovered, concretely, the solidarity of the colonialist bloc and the necessary interdependence of the liberation movements.

The shaking of British imperialism, for example, cannot really be accompanied by a consolidation of French imperialism. In the immediate, such a result may appear obvious. In reality, the national flow, the emergence of new states, prepare and precipitate the inevitable ebb of the international colonialist cohort. The advent of peoples, unknown only yesterday, onto the stage of history, their determination to participate in the building of a civilization that has its place in the world of today give to the contemporary period a decisive importance in the world process of humanization.

The Bandung pact concretizes this carnal and spiritual union at one and the same time. Bandung is the historic commitment of the oppressed to help one another and to impose a definitive setback upon the forces of exploitation.

Algeria a "guide territory"

The Algerian war occupies a choice place in the process of demolition of imperialism. For four years French colonialism, one of the most obstinate in this post-war period, has clung by every means to its bridgehead in Africa. All the military and political arguments have been used to justify the repression and the French presence in Algeria. The dimensions of this atrocious war have amazed and shocked international opinion. French colonialism in Algeria has mobilized all its forces.

The military, economic, and political effort put forth by France in the Algerian war can be evaluated objectively only in relation to the whole "French" Africa. Quelling the Algerian Revolution would of course mean expurgating the "national ferment" for another dozen years. But it would at the same time mean imposing silence on any possible African movements of liberation and, especially, would mark the young Tunisian and Moroccan independencies with the seal of debility and insecurity.

French colonialism in Algeria has considerably enriched the history of barbarous methods used by international colonialism. For the first time we witness the mobilization of several classes, the sending of contingents, the diminution of the forces of national defense, for the benefit of a war of colonial reconquest.

Several times the French authorities have announced an imminent victory over the Algerian national forces. All the objective conditions seemed to be combined to bring about this defeat of the Algerian revolution. Each time there occurred a kind of miracle of renewal, a fresh start.

This is because the Algerian people knows that it has the support of immense international democratic forces. Moreover, the Algerian masses are conscious of the importance of their combat to the African continent as a whole.

The Algerian war is far from ended and at the dawn of this fifth year of war the men and women of Algeria, gripped by an incoercible hunger for peace, lucidly measure the very difficult road they still have to travel. But the positive, decisive, irreversible results that their struggle has just made possible in Africa sustain their faith and strengthen their combativity.

Whereas Tunisia and Morocco, as protectorates, were able to reach independence without fundamentally challenging the French empire, Algeria, by its status, the length of the occupation, and the extent of the colonialist foothold, raises in broad daylight and in a critical fashion the question of the collapse of the empire.

For French colonialism, Algeria is not solely a new colonial conflict but also the occasion of a decisive confrontation, the final test. For this reason the French forces have reacted in the course of this conflict with a brutality and a violence that have often been disconcerting. The Franco-Algerian conflict has presented the colonial problem on the scale of Africa. The other colonial powers in Africa follow the evolution of the Algerian war with anxiety and terror. And now at the other end of the Sahara, independent Guinea is casting her "subversive" shadow in the direction of the best-held territories.

Algeria, the bridgehead of Western colonialism in Africa, has rapidly become the hornet's nest in which French imperialism has got itself stuck and in which the insensate hopes of the Western oppressors have been swallowed up.

The Algerian war has for four years dominated in a tragic

and decisive way the political life of France both at home and abroad. The relations of France with the other Western countries, its diplomatic or sometimes military difficulties with the Arab states, the evolution of the colonialist structures of the old French Union, reflect very clearly the different phases of the Algerian war.

Obsessed by the terror of new colonial wars, French politicians have multiplied warnings and invitations: let us review our problems with our colonial possessions—such is the phrase that has rung out in the French assemblies and political circles since 1955. Mr. Defferre's *Loi-Cadre* was created with a view to avoiding untimely demands for national independence.

But the existence of the Algerian war, the details that have leaked out concerning the colonialist repression, the heroism of the Algerian people, have awakened and emboldened the conscience of the men and women of Africa.

In early 1958, in all the African territories occupied by France, the national will made itself felt and more and more numerous and more and more determined parties faced the necessary problem of armed struggle.

In Togo and the Cameroon, events did in fact assume the aspect of a masked war. Elsewhere the wardens of colonialism abound in mollifying assurances. But beneath these soft words the observer readily detects an intense anxiety and a terror of the people's anger.

The Algerian war has shaken the colonial equilibrium in Africa to its foundations. There is not one occupied territory in Africa that has not modified its future prospects in the light of the Algerian war. The Algerian people is conscious of the importance of the combat in which it is engaged. Since 1954 it has maintained the slogan of the national liberation of Algeria and the liberation of the African continent. The facile criticisms directed against the rigid refusal to accept the stages in decolonization periodically proposed to the FLN do not take the originally African dimensions of the Algerian national struggle sufficiently into account.

French colonialism must die

The appeal to General de Gaulle, under these conditions, was the last venture of French colonialism. We have seen that General de Gaulle could only make the most of a movement which he cannot control. The new constitution, in its discussion on the community, still leaves the metropolis a favored place, but admits the indispensable recognition of autonomous states. The creation of the Madagascan Republic is the first manifestation of this Gaullist reform.

The colonialist circles who had confidently placed their hopes in the providential general's intercession are beginning to wonder today if they have not made a fool's bargain. Having failed to draw the conclusions from an irreversible need which, if it were not satisfied, might well overwhelm France herself, the French colonialists tend to consider de Gaulle as a traitor or as a peddler. As a matter of fact, the general is once again saving the colonialist interests by laying out a community which, being unequal, organized for the sole profit of a metropolis, maintains important colonial structures intact.

With the constitution of autonomous states, French colonialism emerges in a weakened state. But, had it not been for General de Gaulle's intervention, the collapse of the empire would very shortly have ensued. An apparent traitor to his trust, General de Gaulle is in reality the momentary savior of a certain colonial reality.

15

Algeria in Accra

The Algerian delegation composed of five members has received an enthusiastic welcome in Accra. The warm reception testifies to the importance that the African peoples have attached for several years to Algeria's struggle for independence.

We have discovered in Accra that the great figures of the Algerian Revolution—Ben Bella, Ben M'Hidi, Djamila Bouhired—have become a part of the epic of Africa.

A special place has been made for several members of our delegation. One of us has been on the Steering Committee of the Congress and all the others were elected by acclamation to the chairmanship or the vice-chairmanship of the various committees.

Such unanimity with respect to fighting Algeria has manifestly displeased the colonialists, who like to think that the struggle of the Algerian people has awakened no echo among the men and women of Africa south of the Sahara. In reality, the Algerian Revolution has never been so acutely and so substantially present as in this region of Africa; whether among the Senegalese, the Cameroonians, or the South Africans, it was easy to recognize the existence of a fundamental solidarity of these peoples with the struggle of the Algerian people, its methods and its objectives.

The Algerian delegation has presented the problem of the armed struggle very clearly before the Congress members. Certain observers, certain newspapermen in the first hours of the

Congress took it upon themselves to cable to their papers that Algeria had decided to wage the anti-colonialist combat by peaceful methods.

Some of them did not even hesitate to imply that the Algerian revolutionary movement was being officially condemned.

The truth of the matter is that from the first day, the Congress got into its authentic orbit and the Algerian struggle became both the weak point of the colonial system and the rampart of the African peoples.

This was because the Congress members quickly convinced themselves that the interest of the colonialists in Africa and the initial moves in the direction of decolonization that have appeared here and there are not due to the generosity or the sudden intelligence of the oppressors.

The Algerian war has in fact had a decisive bearing on this Congress. For the first time, it was realized, a colonialism waging war in Africa proves itself powerless to win. It is because they had failed to analyze this phenomenon that the colonialists were once again caught off guard and astonished by the success of the Algerian representatives.

Every Algerian delegate was received as one who is expelling the fear, the trembling, the inferiority complex, from the flesh of the colonized.

The struggle of the Algerian people is not saluted as an act of heroism but as a continuous, sustained action, constantly being reinforced, which contains in its development the collapse and the death of French colonialism in Africa.

Guinea was likewise applauded, but was particularly applauded as being the first important consequence of the Franco-Algerian conflict.

The comrade ministers of Guinea present at the Conference have asked us to communicate to our government the deep gratitude of the Guinean people to fighting Algeria.

Moreover, the prime minister of Ghana, Dr. N'Krumah, made a point of receiving our delegates among the first. For more than one hour the Algerian problem in its relation to the liberation of the African continent was studied. Once again the Ghanaian Chief of State pledged the support and the active solidarity of the people of Ghana and of its government to the fighting people of Algeria.

Dr. N'Krumah announced to us the intention of his government to recognize the Provisional Government of the Algerian Republic in the immediate future.

16

Accra: Africa Affirms Its Unity and Defines Its Strategy

In 1884 the Western nations meeting in Berlin decided to divide the African continent and laid the legal foundation for the colonial regime.

Since then the evolution of competing forces on the world's checkerboard, the birth of new powers, have obliged the Western nations to retreat and to withdraw from a large part of their possessions.

After Asia, Africa

Asia is now liberated from colonialism and territories like China, afflicted, it seemed, until now with an absolute wretchedness, are creating a new kind of civilization, an authentic one, which concerns man and which opens limitless prospects for his enhancement.

The fact remains that the African continent is still extensively occupied by the colonial powers and after Bandung, after the Cairo Afro-Asiatic conference, the African peoples have now met in Accra, the capital of independent Ghana, to lay the foundations of a tactic and a strategy of combat with the distant prospect of a United States of Africa.

A "biological" solidarity

The meeting in Accra brought together the political and trade union organizations of the African continent. Their common ideology was a national will opposed to foreign domination; their tactic, to weaken the colonizers one after another;

El Moudjahid, No. 34, December 24, 1958.

their strategy, to frustrate the oppressor's maneuvers and attempts at camouflage.

What struck the observer at Accra was the existence at the most spontaneous level of a solidarity that is organic, even biological. But above this kind of affective communion there was the concern to affirm an identity of objectives and also the determination to use all existing means to banish colonialism from the African continent.

These men and these women had met in order to expose the nature of the colonialism to which they were subject, to study the possible types of struggle, to articulate their offensives, to exert pressure, finally, in territory after territory, on identical colonialisms.

This is why very quickly, outside the commissions, contacts were created among countries under trusteeship, settlement colonies of the South Africa type, Kenya, Algeria, states in the Community represented essentially by the so-called French Africas.

The independent states of Africa received an enthusiastic welcome in Accra. It was these states that had decided, in April 1958, that this meeting in Accra was essential to hasten the liberation of the African continent.

The UAR, Tunisia, Ghana, Ethiopia, etc. had been anxious to delegate to the Congress men and women who bore witness to the unconditional support of those states to the different peoples engaged in struggle.

The young Guinean Republic represented by three of its ministers was enthusiastically acclaimed by the Congress.

Violence and non-violence: the end and the means

Several problems were debated in the course of this conference.

The two most important ones seem to have been the question of non-violence and the question of collaboration with the previously dominating nation.

The problems are obviously linked. The end of the colonial

regime effected by peaceful means and made possible by the colonialist's understanding might under certain circumstances lead to a renewed collaboration of the two nations. History, however, shows that no colonialist nation is willing to withdraw without having exhausted all its possibilities of maintaining itself.

Raising the problem of a non-violent decolonization is less the postulation of a sudden humanity on the part of the colonialist than believing in the sufficient pressure of the new ratio of forces on an international scale.

It is clear, for example, that France has initiated a process of decolonization in Africa south of the Sahara.

This innovation without violence has been made possible by the successive setbacks to French colonialism in the other territories. However, the representatives of the African nations under French domination present in Accra have denounced with lucidity the maneuvers of French imperialism.

The snares of neo-colonialism

The Congress members unreservedly condemned the Africans who, in order to maintain themselves, have not feared to mobilize the police for purposes of rigging the elections in the last referendum and to commit their territories to an association with France which excludes the way of independence for many years. The few delegates who came to represent these puppet governments of French Africa found themselves more or less expelled from the commissions.

On the other hand the representatives of Cameroon [French], with Dr. Félix Moumié at their head, were warmly applauded in the course of the last Session of the UN. Other territories have wrung their independence on a deferred basis: Cameroon [British], Tanganyika, Somaliland.

In 1960, nearly 60 million Africans will again be independent.

Moreover, alarmed by the convulsions that are shaking Africa and by the hardening of the nationalist movements in the

Belgian Congo, the Belgian government has officially recognized the Belgian Congo's claim to independence and proposes in the month of January to present a program by stages for the independence of 20 million Congolese.

It is not excluded that the Belgian colonialists may once again try to retard this date; the Congolese masses must take it upon themselves to impose the Democratic Republic of the Congo at a not too distant date.

If Belgium, England with Nigeria and Tanganyika, France with Guinea have pulled back, Portugal on the contrary is developing a police regime in its possessions. The delegates of Angola were welcomed fervently and an immense anger made itself felt when the assembly was told of the discriminatory and inhuman measures resorted to by the Portuguese authorities. Quite obviously Angola, South Africa, and Algeria are the citadels of colonialism and probably the territories in which the European settlers are defending themselves with the greatest frenzy and ferocity.

In this connection it must be pointed out that the Union of South Africa is attempting to annex Basutoland, Swaziland, and to make junction with the Rhodesias, those other settlers' colonies.

These successive colonizations are certainly one of the most remarkable phenomena of this period of liberation of the continent.

The African legion

In the settlement of colonies of the type of Kenya, Algeria, and South Africa there is unanimity: only armed struggle will bring about the defeat of the occupying nation. And the African legion, the principle of which was adopted in Accra, is the concrete response of the African peoples to the will to colonial domination of the Europeans.

In deciding to create a corps of volunteers in all the territories the African peoples mean clearly to manifest their solidarity with one another, thus expressing the realization that national liberation is linked to the liberation of the continent.

The peoples engaged in struggle, who today are convinced that their African brothers share their combat and are ready to intervene directly at the first call of the directing bodies, contemplate the future in a more serene and optimistic light.

In the popular meetings organized in Ghana, in Ethiopia, in Nigeria, hundreds of men have pledged themselves to come to the aid of the Algerian or South African brothers whenever these manifest such a wish.

Africa must be free, said Dr. N'Krumah in his inaugural speech, we have nothing to lose but our chains and we have an immense continent to win. In Accra, the Africans pledged fidelity and assistance to one another. No alliance will be rejected; the future of colonialism has never been so dark as on the morrow of the Accra Conference.

17

Mr. Debré's Desperate Endeavors

Mr. Michel Debré, head of the French government, recently made a trip to Algeria. He contacted the colonialist authorities and defined for their benefit the program of his government.

"The authority of France in Algeria," he said, "is a requirement of history, of nature, of morality." This statement was illuminated by even firmer pronouncements, like the following sentence spoken before the veterans: "All Algerians must know and understand once and for all that every inhabitant of this country is a French citizen by the same right as any citizen of the metropolis and that in any case the government will not countenance any challenging of this citizenship." And in this other statement, "The truth is that Algeria is a land of French sovereignty," the French prime minister indicated both the unchanged character and mood of the French population in Algeria and the importance of the gap that exists at the present time between the national will of the Algerian people and French colonialist obstinacy.

A falsified historic time

Mr. Debré's program belongs to an eminently orthodox colonialist dogmatism.

Conquest, it is affirmed, creates historic links. The new time inaugurated by the conquest, which is a colonialist time because occupied by colonialist values, because deriving its *raison d'être* from the negation of the national time, will be endowed with an absolute coefficient. The history of the conquest, the historic development of the colonization and of the national spoliation, will be substituted for the real time of the exploited men. And what is affirmed by the colonized at the time of the struggle for national liberation as the will to break with exploitation and contempt will be rejected by the colonialist power as a symbol of barbarism and of regression.

The colonialist, by a process of thinking which is after all fairly commonplace, reaches the point of no longer being able to imagine a time occurring without him. His irruption into the history of the colonized people is deified, transformed into absolute necessity. Now a "historic look at history" requires, on the contrary, that the French colonialist retire, for it has become historically necessary for the national time in Algeria to exist.

Mr. Debré's historical interpretation is the intellectualized equivalent of the old colonialist formula: "It is we who have made Algeria."

What passes itself off as fidelity to history is in the last analysis only infidelity to history, a refusal to measure up to the period of decolonization, disobedience to history.

In 1959 the sense of history requires that the 10 million Algerians take their destiny into their own hands. For more than four years the successive French governments have proved themselves incapable of interpreting this problem objectively. Mr. Debré's statements differ in no way from those uttered by Mr. Léonard or Mr. Soustelle when they said in 1954: "France is in Algeria and means to stay there."

In 1959 the slogan is: "France will remain."

Another theme is generally mentioned by the doctrinaires of colonialism, and that is the theme of the indissoluble union of Algeria and France.

A geography of intentions

Since it can be neither sentimental nor intellectual, this union will be geographic. And France will at times find herself to be the European prolongation of Algeria, while at other times Algeria will be the African prolongation of France.

The international difficulties of Europe will give a more and more marked primacy to this geographic union. Within the framework of the defensive system of the Occident the Algerian territory occupies a privileged place. This is brought out by the various defenders of French Algeria. It is in this light, too, that the problem is mentioned by Mr. Debré: "We must understand, besides, that freedom and progress, security and peace, are linked in this part of the world to the unity, above the Mediterranean, of metropolitan France, the gateway of Europe, and of Algeria, at the head of Africa. Any threat to this unity is a risk of insecurity! Any strengthening of this unity is a pledge of peace. France therefore owes it to herself to see to it that no one can doubt her will to make this unity firmer than ever."

So Algeria must remain French soil because the strategic necessities of Europe and of France require it. Mr. Debré's geography is thus a geography animated with intentions: the authority of France in Algeria is a requirement of nature. It is the natural order that imposes upon France the maintenance of the colonial regime in Algeria. The moment regimes or men begin to read their political actions into the sinuosities of the terrain, we are in the presence of fascism and Nazism.

It is by prolonging in their imagination certain links of terrain that governments menace the world's peace. Let them really give free rein to their fantasies and extend what for centuries have been called natural frontiers, and we have whole peoples steeped in blood and misery.

The geography of Algeria—and this should be a secret to no one—requires first of all that this country be independent.

And after this, to be sure, it has its place in the Maghreb, in Africa, and in the world. But to deny the national destiny of Algeria in the name of a "great Franco-Algerian union" is sheer imposture. In this Mr. Debré does not innovate. For four years the traditions have been established in the French governments.

Eluding history and nature, Mr. Debré emerges upon morality. Here again, apparently without effort, he rediscovers the great principles of ultra-colonialism: "What will the Algerians do without us?" The settlers of the Mitidja used to say, and still say: "These vineyards, in four years, will turn into swamps."

What Mr. Debré says is no different: "They want to give Algeria over to wretchedness, barbarism, and drown it in blood."

Morality to the rescue of exploitation

Now—and this is another theme—only France is capable of taking Algeria in charge beneficially.

Only France can take charge of Algeria economically.

All this Mr. Debré is to repeat in Algiers.

"France has an obligation of an economic order. . . . France has an obligation of a social order. . . . France has a human obligation, for she alone is capable of maintaining and of strengthening . . . this union and this brotherhood of spirits that give to Algeria a character and a force that are unique in the world."

A sign of the times! At the beginning of the conquest, it was this pretext that was invoked. A fight against barbarism, poverty, backwardness. Today, after 130 years of exploitation, which paradoxically constitute a right, and the fight between blocs, it is history and strategy that take the first rank.

French morality, French values are alone capable of maintaining Algeria in the camp of "human regions." The departure of France, Mr. Debré warns us, would be the sign of a relapse of Algeria into archaism, backwardness, and idiocy.

Eight months after the seizure of power by General de Gaulle, we are now back to the first months of our people's struggle for liberation. "France is at home in Algeria, for Algeria is France's achievement. France needs Algeria, for without Algeria what would France do? Algeria needs France, for without France what would Algeria do?"

And to conclude, this detail contained in Mr. Debré's personal speech: "Who, but evil minds, with ulterior motives, can doubt General de Gaulle's resolutions? Who, but evil spirits, with ulterior motives, dare have doubts when General de Gaulle has stated that there would be no political negotiations?"

The Fifth French Republic seems to give evidence of no greater imagination than the preceding one. The same affirmations are repeated with the same blind obstinacy, the same contempt for events, the same grasp of history.

To claim in 1959 that all Algerians are French, that France will remain in Algeria and that political negotiations are ruled out, is to commit oneself, against common sense, to the path of intensification of the war.

It is undeniably turning one's back on negotiation and on reason.

It is true that this blindness is not the result of a mistaken judgment. France and its government are still dominated by colonialist interests. Since the 13th of May we have witnessed the alliance of these traditional interests with the fascist and militarist trend, which has always been very strong in France (Boulanger, de la Roque, Pétain . . .) and a certain fraction of the major financial interests.

So long as this alliance is not challenged, the French prime ministers are condemned to find the source of inspiration for their statements in the ultra-colonialist tradition.

There should be no mistake about the fact that it will be a long time before the colonialist coalition bursts asunder, through the development of contradictions.

Today, as throughout the past four years, the slogan is still to intensify the armed struggle. All attempts at diversion by the adversary must be quelled.

The conditions for a negotiation are far from having been met on the French side. Mr. Debré's program is to wage war, to deny the Algerian nation, to extend the annexation of our country.

Yes, as Mr. Yazid, the Minister of Information, said, to speak of French sovereignty in Algeria in 1959 is madness. There is no other word.

18

Racist Fury in France

Two years ago, as a result of the action of ALN commandos on French territory, whether to neutralize the then very active counter-revolution, or to react against certain torturers of the French police, spontaneous attitudes of racism and passionate discrimination against North Africans were seen to develop. In an immediate and inclusive way suspicion of the Arabs became second nature. One step more and the hunt was on. This was the period, it may be remembered, when even a South American was riddled with bullets, because he looked like a North African.

Tunisian and Moroccan citizens were to suffer equally from this racist behavior. Tunisian workers were arrested, interned, given the third degree . . . Moroccan students were apprehended, grilled in the headquarters of the judicial police . . . In the streets it was common to hear remarks that were disagreeable and humiliating both to the young states and to the individuals who were their citizens.

This was the period, it will be remembered, when every North African was repeatedly challenged and when numerous Tunisian or Moroccan workers working in France decided to return to their national territory.

It was at this time that it became the habit to decree that only the Algerians were responsible for this state of things and that it was up to the Algerians to put an end to this general suspicion with regard to the North African population.

Thus this highly aggressive and hateful behavior was not a component of the social and mental structure of the French people, but simply the defense reaction of an organism that could not readily distinguish the various inhabitants of the Maghreb.

The recent events that have occurred on French territory deserve to be mentioned here. They will show us beyond any doubt that the confusion in the perception of the "furriner" was not to be attributed to a regrettable ignorance, but had its justification in a principle, a commonplace one, according to which the crudest forms of race-discrimination are making headway in France at a truly explosive rate.

A writer stabbed

The first fact is the attack on the young writer Oyono, three weeks ago. The author of *Une Vie de Boy* was coming out of a restaurant in the company of a woman. The couple was assaulted, the woman insulted in an obscene fashion, slapped in the face, trampled on. As for Oyono, after having resisted his assailants, he collapsed, with a dagger between his shoulderblades. He was rushed to a Paris hospital, was given a blood transfusion, and eventually recovered. Now up and about, he freely admits that he does not feel safe on French territory and is preparing to leave.

How is one to interpret this event? This is not an attack aimed at a colored man, not an attempted robbery. As the perpetrators made no secret of proclaiming, this was a punishment inflicted on the woman (who was white), and a warning administered to the Negro. The gang fell on Oyono, shouting, "*A mort les nègres!*"

Before he fainted, Oyono was able to identify for the police one of his assailants. Their names, to this day, have not been made known and despite the firm position taken by several organizations it is doubtful that the case will ever come to court. It should be pointed out that the event occurred right in the Latin Quarter, in other words in the very center of the intellectual quarter accustomed to the presence of students of every nationality. No one came to the aid of the victim and, when the operation was over, the assailants were quietly allowed to vanish.

An anti-racist film under attack . . .

A number of films have recently been made to combat the racism that is rife in the United States and elsewhere. The most recent of these, *Tripes au soleil,* of which there is a great deal to be said, has just been shown in Paris. At the very first showing some young Parisians created a deafening pandemonium, broke chairs, soiled the screen with refuse, and manifested their hostility at the end of the showing. Cries of "Down with Negroes!" "Death to Negroes!" "Long live Hitler!" were shouted, and the police "dispersed the demonstrators."

For several weeks, in a systematic way, anti-fascist organizations have been under attack. One of the most active movements, the MRAP,[1] against racism, anti-semitism, and in favor of peace, which was one of the first to take a position against the principle of the Algerian war and for the recognition of the Algerian nation, is constantly being attacked. Its headquarters are broken into almost daily and its leading members subjected to threats and acts of violence. In the past several weeks, too, swastikas have made their appearance on Paris walls. These hooked crosses are but replicas of those that have been in evidence for a longer time in Algiers and in Constantine.

When it is possible in France for an anti-racist film to be attacked in broad daylight by an organization that does not fear to proclaim the slogan, "Death to Negroes!" it can be said that democracy in France is in a bad way and that Negroes would do well to leave the ship.

But then, it will be said, must one not be careful not to generalize from these facts?

Are these not simply episodic manifestations forbidden by law and unanimously condemned by the French national conscience? Perhaps we must look into this a little more closely.

---

[1] MRAP—*Mouvement Contre le Racisme et l'Antisémitisme et pour la Paix.* —*Tr.*

And perhaps such manifestations do not arise spontaneously. For them to exist, for them to take shape, there must have developed a sufficient sedimentation of racism, of superiority complex, of discrimination in this very national conscience. These manifestations, sprung straight from the heart, that is to say from the heart of the individual, express both the vice of French education with respect to the rest of humanity, and the consequences of decades of colonial domination.

Did not General de Gaulle himself, in his last speech in Blois, miraculously rediscover this way to the heart?

Speaking of the necessity to reach an understanding in Europe, did he not say, "We whites, we civilized men, owe it to ourselves to reach a common ground of understanding"?

One is inevitably reminded of this passage from the Negro poet, Césaire: "What he [the twentieth-century bourgeois humanist] does not forgive Hitler is not the crime in itself, the crime against the white man, it is the inflicting on Europeans of European colonialist procedures which until now were reserved for the Arabs of Algeria, the coolies of India, and the Negroes of Africa."

Yes, when racism in France reaches such dimensions, it is time for Negroes to leave the ship. It is up to the members of the "French Community" to decide whether their place is still by the side of those who have not yet rid themselves either of indignities or of hatred toward the black race.

19

Blood Flows in the
Antilles Under French Domination

So now the old colonies, too, are taking the road to "rebellion." Those ornaments of the empire, those castrated countries that gave such good and loyal servants are beginning to stir.

Every West Indian, every Guianan, wherever he may find himself today, will feel violently shaken. Indeed the French, after having categorized the Arabs and the Africans, the Madagascans and the Indochinese, in a pejorative way, recognized that with the West Indians things took on a different character. The West Indians, one was told on all sides, are French, like the Corsicans. And there were enormous masses of West Indians, men and women, who believed it. To be sure, race prejudice would break out from time to time; to be sure, the West Indian settler class oppressed and condemned the agricultural workers to endemic famine, but the title of French citizen was surely worth these few unpleasantnesses. To be sure, three hundred tons of gold left the Guianan territory every year to fill the cellars of the Banque de France, but was not Mr. Monnerville,[1] as the second or third in rank of French citizens, both a symbol and the payment of a debt?

Yet despite this great intoxication, despite this enormous imposture, there were Martiniquans who entered into open struggle against the French forces, who blockaded commissariats, who cut roads. Submerging those three hundred years of French presence there were Martiniquans who brought out

El Moudjahid, No. 58, January 5, 1960.
[1] Gaston Mannerville, President of the Council of the French Republic, was born in French Guiana.

their arms and occupied Fort-de-France for more than six hours. There were people killed. And wounded too.

Fifteen dead, we are told, several dozen wounded, and hundreds of arrests.

Reinforcements have been sent to the Antilles and in order to halt a movement which must appear fairly imminent Guadeloupe is being flooded with marines, members of the CRS[2] and soldiers.

The French information services claim that the origin of the riot was a commonplace traffic incident. Perhaps. But then why suddenly these extensive measures? How does it happen that a population reacts with such violence, such rage? How does it happen that the CRS reacts with such precipitation, with so little concern for the lives of "fellow-citizens"?

In reality the problem has been raised. And this is all to the good. The fiction of the French Antilles, the formula, "for the West Indian there is no problem," is now again challenged. And this is all to the good.

The old politicians, assimilated, harassed from within, who for a long time represented only their own mediocre interests and their own mediocrity, must today be very worried. They suddenly discover that the people of Martinique can perfectly well be treated as rebels by France. They are also discovering the existence of a rebellious spirit, of a national spirit.

At the time of the referendum organized by France, Césaire had been asked the reason for his "Yes" to de Gaulle. It was, he replied, because the people of Martinique had made a wager with the Fifth Republic. Our "Yes," Césaire said, is a conditional "Yes." France undertakes to improve our condition and to grant us certain prerogatives on a local level.

Well! It seems that the people have challenged this wager and raised the national problem. The West Indian question, the question of the Caribbean federation, can no longer be disre-

---

[2] CRS—*Compagnie Républicaine de Sécurité*, a national constabulary army corps independent of the regular army.—*Tr.*

garded. The ex-Dutch and ex-British Guianas, which are today independent, exert an attraction on Guiana under French domination. The West Indies under British domination obtain their independence. Castro in Cuba has given the Caribbean a new look. Yes, the question is raised.

At this time, the French forces and their allies, the present politicians, deputies, and senators, will undoubtedly break this first manifestation of the national spirit of Martinique. But we know now that the people of Guadeloupe, of Martinique, and of Guiana will be independent and will build their respective countries as they see fit. The Algerian people assures the West Indians and the people of Guiana of its brotherly sympathy and encourages them to sharpen their combativity. The West Indian and Guianan soldiers, non-coms and officers who are fighting against their Algerian brothers while the French troops machine-gun their peoples in Fort-de-France or in Basse Terre, must refuse to fight and desert.

We know now that there are links between the Algerian war and the recent events that have caused blood to be shed in Martinique. It is former French civil servants of North Africa, those who were expelled from Morocco, from Tunisia, and those who were too compromised in Algeria, who have provoked the retaliation of the Martinique masses. The violent reaction of the people of Martinique simply indicates that the time has come to clarify problems and to dissipate misunderstandings.

20

Unity and Effective Solidarity Are the Conditions for African Liberation

For an observer who has followed the evolution of the African continent for two years, one conclusion is particularly obvious: the dependent peoples on whom foreign domination weighs are progressively achieving national sovereignty.

After Ghana and Guinea, now the Cameroon under French mandate, Togoland, Somaliland under Italian mandate, Nigeria are becoming independent. The stirrings that agitate the recent French community, the outspoken—or sometimes veiled—demands voiced by the leaders of the different countries of the community, allow of no doubt. A process has begun which, if one could trust stereotyped formulas, might be called irreversible.

The hand of history is the hand of man

An outside observer might therefore limit his awareness to the generalized hope in the historic development of what has been called the objective process of decolonization, whereas Africans are being asked more or less explicitly to put their confidence in the good will of the former masters and not to despair, in any case, of the historic necessities that dictate the tempo of the reconversion of colonial oppression.

It is rigorously true that decolonization is proceeding, but it is rigorously false to pretend and to believe that this decolonization is the fruit of an objective dialectic which more or less rapidly assumes the appearance of an absolutely inevitable mechanism.

El Moudjahid, No. 58, January 5, 1960.

The optimism that prevails today in Africa is not an optimism born of the spectacle of forces of nature that are at last favorable to Africans. Nor is the optimism due to the discovery in the former oppressor of a less inhuman and more kindly state of mind. Optimism in Africa is the direct product of the revolutionary action of the African masses, whether political or armed —often both at one and the same time.

We understand now why every African nationalist is so obsessed with constantly giving an African dimension to his action. This is because the struggle for freedom and national independence is dialectically linked to the struggle against colonialism in Africa.

The enemy of the African under French domination is not colonialism insofar as it exerts itself within the strict limits of his nation, but it is the forms of colonialism, it is the manifestations of colonialism, whatever be the flag under which it asserts itself.

A large part of humanity has recently trembled to the very depth of its being before the breaking loose of an ideology, Nazism, which revived the methods of torture and genocide of the remotest times.

The countries against which the manifestations of Nazism were most immediately directed leagued together and pledged themselves not only to liberate their occupied territories but literally to break the backbone of Nazism, to root out the evil where it had sprung up, to liquidate the regimes to which it had given rise.

Well! The African peoples must likewise remember that they have had to face a form of Nazism, a form of exploitation of man, of physical and spiritual liquidation clearly imposed, that the French, English, and South African manifestations of that evil need to engage their attention, but they must be prepared also to face this evil as an evil extending over the whole of the African territory.

The European countries are today concerned with the problem of peace. After having armed themselves to the teeth, the

Eastern and Western blocs perceive with terror that any new world conflict would endanger the very existence of life on earth. For this reason a peaceful confrontation of the two world conceptions becomes indispensable.

It was with this in mind that General Eisenhower undertook his last tour abroad, that the NATO council met in Paris, and that a summit meeting has been arranged for the first months of 1960.

We Africans say that the problem of peace among men—non-African, in the present instance—is fundamental, but we also say that the liberation of Africa, of the last bastions of colonialism, constitutes the first problem.

When we Africans say that we are neutral on the relations between East and West, we mean that for the time being the only question that concerns us is our fight against colonialism. This means that we are absolutely not neutral in respect to genocide being carried out by France in Algeria, or to *apartheid* in South Africa.

Our neutrality means that we do not have to take a position for or against NATO, for or against the Warsaw pact.

Within the framework of our anti-colonialist combat, we take into account only the firmness of our commitment and the backing that this or that country gives us. And within this framework we can say that the peoples grouped under the label of Eastern countries are giving us very strong support and that the so-called countries of the West are full of ambiguities.

Arms and the man

The African peoples are concretely involved in a total struggle against colonialism, and we Algerians do not dissociate the combat we are waging from that of the Rhodesians or the Kenyans. Our solidarity toward our African brothers is not merely verbal. It does not express itself through a vote, through acclamation in an international meeting of resolutions or condemnations. The colonialist countries, when they were in danger, and fascism, Nazism were submerging them, hence when their freedom and their independence were threatened, did not hesitate to tap the African masses and to hurl a majority of the "colonials" against the Nazi positions. Today it is the freedom and independence of the Africans that are at issue.

The inter-African solidarity must be a solidarity of fact, a solidarity of action, a solidarity concrete in men, in equipment, in money.

Africa shall be free. Yes, but it must get to work, it must not lose sight of its own unity. It is in this spirit that one of the most important among a number of points at the first Congress of African peoples in Accra in 1958 was adopted. The African peoples, it was said in that resolution, pledge themselves to create a militia which will have the duty to support the African peoples fighting for their independence.

It is not by chance that this resolution was conjured out of sight by the Western press. The violence of the Western democracies during their war against Nazism, the violence of the United States at Hiroshima with the atom bomb, without serving as an example, give a measure of what the democracies can do when their existence is in danger.

We Africans say that for more than 100 years the life of 200 million Africans has been life at a discount, contested, a life perpetually haunted by death. We say that we must not trust to the good faith of the colonialists, but that we must arm ourselves with firmness and combativeness. Africa will not be free through the mechanical development of material forces, but it is the hand of the African and his brain that will set into motion and implement the dialectics of the liberation of the continent.

A few days from the Second Conference of African peoples that is to be held at the gates of Algeria as it is being put to fire and sword, the Africans must remember that there is not an objective optimism that is more or less mechanically inevitable, but that optimism must be the sentiment that accompanies the revolutionary commitment and the combat.

Under these conditions, yes, we can be optimistic.

V

African Unity

1

This Africa to Come

[At the end of the year 1958 the *wilaya* colonels of the ALN held a meeting in the Nord-Constantinois. On this occasion they took note of the danger of a progressive strangling of the armed struggle in the interior as a result of the disposition of the enemy forces (forbidden areas, regrouping camps tending to cut off the ALN from the population).

It was decided to send Colonel Amirouche (colonel of *wilaya* III) to Tunis to explain the situation to the GPRA (Provisional Government of the Algerian Republic) and define the means whereby the interior could be supplied with arms, munitions, and finances.

Colonel Amirouche never reached Tunis, for he was killed by the enemy during this voyage in the region of Bou-Saâda in March 1959.

It was in order to meet this situation that the CNRA (National Committee of the Algerian Revolution) decided at its meeting in the fall of 1959 to create the General Staff.

The French army having reinforced its army at the frontiers (the Challe line) it was becoming difficult to supply the interior via Morocco and Tunisia.

In March 1960 Fanon was appointed to Accra. During his stay in West Africa he found that there was a possibility of strengthening the situation within by way of the southern frontier, namely the Mali frontier. He made contact with the Mali authorities and communicated his suggestions to the Algerian leaders who decided to set up a third base south of the Sahara for the shipment of arms to *wilayas* I and V.

The notes that follow were written by Fanon in the course of the mission for the reconnaissance and setting up of this base during the summer of 1960.

To this logbook are added a number of technical problems in the form of hasty and unfinished notes in which Fanon examines the various solutions that might be adopted on the strictly operational level.]

To put Africa in motion, to cooperate in its organization, in its regrouping, behind revolutionary principles. To participate in the ordered movement of a continent—this was really the work I had chosen. The first point of departure, the first base was represented by Guinea. Then Mali, ready for anything, fervent and brutal, coherent and singularly keen, extended the bridgehead and opened valuable prospects. To the East, Lumumba was marking time. The Congo which constituted the second landing beach for revolutionary ideas was caught in an inextricable network of sterile contradictions. The colonialist citadels of Angola, Mozambique, Kenya, the Union of South Africa were not ripe to be effectively blockaded.

Yet everything was set. And here the colonialist system of defense, while discordant, was reviving old particularisms and breaking up the liberating lava. For the moment it was therefore necessary to hang on in the Congo and advance in the West. For us Algerians the situation was clear. But the terrain remained difficult, very difficult. Taking the West as a starting point, we had to prove, by concrete demonstrations, that this continent was one. That behind the general choices of the leaders, it was possible to determine the precise points at which the peoples, the men and the women, could meet, help one another, build in common. The specter of the West, the European tinges, was everywhere present and active. The French, English, Spanish, Portuguese areas remained living. Oxford was opposed to the Sorbonne, Lisbon to Brussels, the English bosses to the Portuguese bosses, the pound to the franc, the Catholic Church to Protestantism or to Islam. And above all this, the United States had plunged in everywhere, dollars in the vanguard, with Armstrong as herald and American Negro diplomats, scholarships, the emissaries of the Voice of America . . . And one must not forget hardworking Germany, Israel reclaiming the desert . . .

A difficult task. Fortunately, in every corner arms make signs to us, voices answer us, hands grasp ours. Things are on the move.

The rapid and reassuring sound of the liberated cities that break their moorings and move forward, grandiloquent but by no means grandiose, these former militants now having definitely passed their examinations who sit down and remember ... But the sun is still very high in the heavens and if one listens with one ear glued to the red earth one very distinctly hears the sound of rusty chains, groans of distress, and the bruised flesh is so constantly present in this stifling noonday that one's shoulders droop with the weight of it. The Africa of everyday, oh not the poets' Africa, the one that puts to sleep, but the one that prevents sleep, for the people is impatient to do, to play, to say. The people that says: I want to build myself as a people, I want to build, to love, to respect, to create. This people that weeps when you say: I come from a country where the women have no children and the children no mothers and that sings: Algeria, brother country, country that calls, country that hopes.

That is the real Africa, the Africa that we had to let loose in the continental furrow, in the continental direction. The Africa that we had to guide, mobilize, launch on the offensive. This Africa to come.

The West. Conakry, Bamako. Two cities dead on the surface, but underneath, the temperature is unendurable for those who calculate, who maneuver, who settle. In Conakry and in Bamako men and women strike Africa, forge it with love and enthusiasm.

Moumié. On September 30th we met on the Accra airfield. He was going to Geneva for some very important meetings. In three months, he told us, we would witness a mass ebbing of colonialism in Cameroon.

In Tripoli, a fog prevented any landing and for three hours the plane circles above the airfield. The pilot wanted to land at any cost. The control tower refused the requested authorization but the courageous and heedless pilot had decided to land his tens of thousands of tons. "Those fellows gamble with people's lives," Félix said to me.

It was true. But were we not also gambling with ours? What was this pilot's intrepidity compared to our lives perpetually in suspense? Today Félix is dead. In Rome, two weeks later, we were to have met again. He was absent. His father standing at the arrival in Accra saw me coming, alone, and a great sadness settled on his face.

Two days later a message told us that Félix was hospitalized. Then that poisoning was suspected. Kingue, the vice-president of the UPC[1] and Marthe Moumié decided to go to Geneva. A few days later the news reached us: Félix Moumié was dead.

We hardly felt this death. A murder, but a bloodless one. There were neither volleys nor machine guns nor bombs. Thallium poisoning. It made no sense. Thallium! How was one to grasp such a cause? An abstract death striking the most concrete, the most alive, the most impetuous man. Félix's tone was constantly high. Aggressive, violent, full of anger, in love with his country, hating cowards and maneuverers. Austere, hard, incorruptible. A bundle of revolutionary spirit packed into 60 kilos of muscle and bone.

In the evening we went to comfort the Cameroon comrades. The father, his face seamed, impassive, inexpressive, listened to me speak of his son. And progressively the father yielded place to the militant. Yes, he said, the program is clear. We must stick to the program. Moumié's father, at that moment, reminded me of those parents in Algeria who listen in a kind of stupor to the story of the death of their children. Who from time to time ask a question, require a detail, then relapse into that inertia of communion that seems to draw them toward where they think their sons have gone.

Action, however, will not be forgotten. Tomorrow, presently, the war must be carried to the enemy, who must be given no rest, pursued, knocked out.

We are off. Our mission: to open the southern front. To transport arms and munitions from Bamako. Stir up the Saharan population, infiltrate to the Algerian high plateaus. After carrying Algeria to the four corners of Africa, move up with all Africa toward African Algeria, toward the North, toward Algiers, the continental city. What I should like: great

[1] UPC—Union of the Populations of the Cameroons.—*Tr.*

lines, great navigation channels through the desert. Subdue the desert, deny it, assemble Africa, create the continent. That Malians, Senegalese, Guineans, Ghanaians should descend from Mali onto our territory. And those of the Ivory Coast, of Nigeria, of Togoland. That they should all climb the slopes of the desert and pour over the colonialist bastion. To turn the absurd and the impossible inside out and hurl a continent against the last ramparts of colonial power.

There are eight of us: a commando, the Army, transmission, political commissars, the sanitary corps. Each of the pairs is to prospect the working possibilities in respect to his own field. We must work fast. Time presses. The enemy is still stubborn. In reality he does not believe in military defeat. But I have never felt it so possible, so within reach. We need only march, and charge. It is not even a question of strategy. We have mobilized furious cohorts, loving our combat, eager to work. We have Africa with us. A continent is getting into motion and Europe is languorously asleep. Fifteen years ago it was Asia that was stirring. Today 650 million Chinese, calm possessors of an immense secret, are building a world by themselves alone. The giving birth of a world.

Chawki. A funny chap. A major in the ALN, born in the Souf. Small, lean, with the implacable eyes of an old *maquis* fighter. Those eyes tell their own story. They say openly that they have witnessed hard things: repressions, tortures, cannon fire, hunts, liquidations . . . One notes in those eyes a kind of haughtiness, of almost murderous hardness. Of non-intimidation too. One quickly forms the habit of paying attention to such men. One can say anything to them but they need to feel and to touch the Revolution in the words uttered. They are very difficult to deceive, to get around.

For the time being Chawki and I share the same bed. Our discussions last rather late into the night and I constantly marvel at the intelligence and the clarity of his ideas. Having received a degree at the Islam University of Zitouna in Tunisia, he wanted to make contact with Western civilization. He settled in Algiers to learn French, to see, judge, discriminate. But the atmosphere of Algiers with the contemptuous settlers, his total ignorance of the French language, the closed nature of the European circles made him decide to go to France. For two years he lived in Paris, mixed in European circles, haunted the libraries and devoured hundred of books.

He finally returned to Algeria and planned to develop his father's land. 1954. He took down his hunting rifle from its hook and joined the brothers. He knows the Sahara like the palm of his hand. When he speaks of that inhuman desert immensity it assumes an infinity of details. Hospitable corners, dangerous roads, mortal regions, points of penetration, the Sahara is a world in which Chawki moves with the boldness and the perspicacity of a great strategist. The French do not suspect the tricks this man is ready to play on them.

Our mission nearly ended in the third-degree rooms of Algeria. From Accra the Ghana Airways clerk, Mensah, who requires some tens of thousands of francs for each reservation, had confirmed our Monrovia-to-Conakry flight. But at the Liberian airport we were told that the plane was full and that we would have to wait till the next day to fly to Conakry by an Air France plane. The employes were abnormally attentive to us and offered to have the company pay all our stop-over expenses. This exemplary solicitude, the French nationality of several of the employes, and the bar-maid allure of a voluble and excruciatingly boring French lady led us to change our route. We decided to leave Monrovia by road and enter Guinea at night via N'Zérékoré.

Until the last moment the employees were convinced that we were taking the plane which was two hours late that day.

The French Intelligence had indeed taken the matter in hand. Instead of heading for Freetown on leaving Robertsfield, the plane turned back and landed at Abidjan where it was searched by French forces.

It is clear that the Ivory Coast government has a prime responsibility in this affair. Such an operation could not have taken place without its connivance or at least its benediction. Houphouët-Boigny, whom certain people try to exonerate, continues to play a leading role in the French colonial system, and the African peoples would have a great deal to gain by isolating him and hastening his downfall. Houphouët-Boigny is objectively the most conscious curb on the evolution and the liberation of Africa. In the end the Intelligence Office had to rue it. Such an operation is a paying proposition only if it succeeds. A public failure under such conditions reveals bandit methods which may cause even those who have been willing to shut their eyes to harden their attitude.

I hope, in any case, that the French authorities have lost track of us.

Here we are in Bamako, the Mali capital. Modibo Keita, ever militant, quickly understands. No need of great speeches. Our working sessions move fast. Without any loss of time the brothers of the Transmission Services discuss with him the problem with which they are concerned and reach the decision to set up a listening post at Kayes. I believe it should be in operation by December 5th. For the time being we are lodged at the rest center of the Bamako barracks. Great agitation these last days. N'Krumah is arriving on the 21st on an official visit.

In Bamako the French element of the population is still considerable. Bookshops, pharmacies, business houses belong in the majority to French settlers. Here and there one comes across a major, a sergeant or two . . . Yesterday, which was Sunday, the 20th, a French adjutant serving in the Mali Army coming from Ségou with a company arrived at the rest center. He introduced himself very politely and shook hands with us. He wanted to know if we could not put a bed at his disposal. One has to have a certain sense of humor about these things. In any case we were able to obtain an armed sentinel who went on duty at eight in the evening. From time to time cars driven by Europeans would cruise round the villa. Not a very safe district. Fortunately things moved fast. On Tuesday the 22nd at five in the morning we left for Gao. The Bamako-Timbuktu road was not passable.

From Bamako we reached Ségou where Jouanelle welcomed us. We refueled and reached San. Then Mopti. At Mopti we hit a snag. As we left town we ran into a police barrier, and the sentinels demanded our passports. There ensued a painful discussion, for in spite of the document issued by the Minister of the Interior the *gendarmes* wanted to check our identities. Finally the chief of the post arrived, and I had of necessity to present myself. But he was not a man to be put off. He wanted to know the nature of our mission and the qualifications of those who accompanied me.

Then I got angry and asked him to hold me and to put me under arrest for refusal to present our papers. Faced with this ultimatum he realized that he had blundered and let us go, at the same time promising absolute secrecy.

The road from Mopti to Douentza is a joke. In the middle of a forest one follows by guess-work the tracks of a car that must have passed there six months before. Such feeling one's way in the middle of the night is very painful and more than once we lost our way. At last, at two in the morning, we arrived. There was no one in the village. The commandant was absent and his wife sent us to the encampment which was closed. We somehow managed, with some in the car, others outside, to get a little rest. At seven we set off for Gao via Hombori. At nine at night we knocked at the commandant's. Ten minutes later we were hard at work. Everything seemed favorable and the Malians were quite determined to help us in creating this third front. People used to speak admiringly of the Odyssey of General Leclerc's march across the Sahara. The one that we are preparing, if the French government does not realize it in time, will make the Leclerc episode look, by comparison, like a Sunday-school picnic. In Gao we found a complete documentation left by the French secret service on the Algerian Moroccan border country. All the names of Algerians living there were mentioned. In the margin were also mentioned their greater or lesser goodwill in respect to nationalist ideas. With no trouble at all we found the negative of the skeleton of a working and transit cell. Thanks to commandant Cardaire.

After two days in Gao we headed for Aguerhoc. The Gao commandant made us take off our peuhl garments and offered each a good Arab scout outfit with a Mas 36 gun and 20 cartridges. We were to have occasion, in fact, to kill a bustard and several does.

In Aguerhoc, at about 11 at night, we met the chief of the Kidal subdivision who was accompanied by the post commander of Tessalit. Introductions all around. Thirty minutes later we were discussing strategy, terrain, passage . . .

It is thrilling to experience these moments. These two officers had only to know who we were to make a whole immense collusion, latent until then, come out into the open. What we want, they give us. Did we want to see at close range the frontier, Tessalit, Bouressa across from Tir Zaouaten where the French, caught short, are building an airfield . . . ? O.K.

And off we were, across 100 kilometers of dirt road. This part of the Sahara is not monotonous. Even the sky up there is constantly changing. Some days ago we saw a sunset that turned the robe of heaven a bright violet. Today it is a very hard red that the eye encounters. Aguerhoc, Tessalit, Bouressa. At Tessalit we cross the French military camp. A French soldier, bared to the waist, gives us a friendly wave. His arms would drop off him if he could guess whom these Arab outfits conceal.

At Bouressa we made contact with a Malian nomad group. We are learning more and more details about the French forces. Bordj le Prieur, Tir Zaouaten, Bidon V.

And, beyond, Tamanrasset where, by piecing things together, we managed to get a fairly exact idea of the French forces. The guides that we found in Bouressa seem reliable and determined. We shall have to give them priority when we need guides later.

In Kidal I plunge into some books on the history of the Sudan. I relive, with the intensity that circumstances and the place confer upon them, the old empires of Ghana, of Mali, of Gao, and the impressive Odyssey of the Moroccan troups with the famous Djouder. Things are not simple. Here Algeria at war comes to solicit aid from Mali. And during this time

Morocco is demanding Mauritania and a part of Mali . . . Also a part of Algeria.

This Saharan region worked over by so many influences and where French officers are constantly creating nests of dissidence we are now preparing to stir to its depths round a battlefield which will require a great deal of rigor and cool thinking. A few observations picked up here and there, with always a special emphasis when Islam and the race is mentioned, require extra caution.

Colonialism and its derivatives do not, as a matter of fact, constitute the present enemies of Africa. In a short time this continent will be liberated. For my part, the deeper I enter into the cultures and the political circles the surer I am that the great danger that threatens Africa is the absence of ideology. Old Europe had toiled for centuries before completing the national unity of the States. And even when a final period could be put to it, how many wars still! With the triumph of socialism in Eastern Europe we witness a spectacular disappearance of the old rivalries, of the traditional territorial claims. That nucleus of wars and political assassinations that Bulgaria, Hungary, Estonia, Slovakia, Albania represented, has made way for a coherent world whose objective is the building of a socialist society.

In Africa, on the other hand, the countries that come to independence are as unstable as their new middle classes or their renovated princes. After a few hesitant steps in the international arena the national middle classes, no longer feeling the threat of the traditional colonial power, suddenly develop great appetites. And as they do not yet have any political experience they think they can conduct political affairs like their business. Perquisites, threats, even despoiling of the victims. All of which is of course regrettable, for the small states have no other choice but to beg the former metropolis to remain just a little longer. In these imperialist pseudo-states, likewise, an extreme militarist policy leads to a reduction of public investments in countries which in certain respects are still medieval. The discontented workers undergo a repression as pitiless as that of the colonial periods. Trade unions and opposition political parties are confined to a quasi-clandestine state. The people, the people who had given everything in the difficult moments of the struggle for national liberation wonder, with their empty hands and bellies, as to the reality of their victory.

For nearly three years I have been trying to bring the misty idea of African Unity out of the subjectivist bogs of the majority of its supporters. African Unity is a principle on the basis of which it is proposed to achieve the United States of Africa without passing through the middle-class chauvinistic national phase with its procession of wars and death-tolls.

To initiate this unity all combinations are possible.

Some, like Guinea, Ghana, Mali, and tomorrow perhaps Algeria, put political action to the forefront. Others like Liberia and Nigeria insist on economic cooperation. The UAR on its side puts more emphasis on the cultural aspect. Everything is possible and the different states should avoid discrediting or denouncing those that see this unity, this coming-together of the African states, in a way that differs from theirs. What must be avoided is the Ghana-Senegal tension, the Somali-Ethiopia, the Morocco-Mauritania, the Congo-Congo tensions . . . In reality the colonized states that have reached independence by the political path seem to have no other concern than to find themselves a real battlefield with wounds and destruction. It is clear, however, that this psychological explanation, which appeals to a hypothetical need for release of pent-up aggressiveness, does not satisfy us. We must once again come back to the Marxist formula. The triumphant middle classes are the most impetuous, the most enterprising, the most annexationist in the world (not for nothing did the French bourgeoisie of 1789 put Europe to fire and sword).

Technical problems

1. Passages by truck: difficult to achieve in the immediate. The thing has to be prepared. Contact the driver. Then study

the process. Study the filling stations. Will require, if one is to provide a minimum of safeguards and ensure a maximum of success, at least three months of preparation from the time the project is really begun.

2. The whole problem is to know whether what is wanted is:
   a) either to supply the forces already in existence in the Sahara;
   b) or supply *wilayas* I, V, and the remains of VI;
   c) or literally create a series of lines of attack perpendicular to the Tellien Atlas which could possibly meet up with and work with the already existing *wilayas*. Of course it can be said that these choices are not mutually exclusive and that these three possibilities can be included in a single program. In any case one of these three possibilities must be given priority even if the Sahara operation as a whole were to contain all three.

Personally I incline to point c.

How is it to be carried out?

Before anything else, bring the maximum of equipment up to the frontier. In the two months to come: 10,000 rifles, 4,000 P.M., 1,500 F.M., 600 machine-guns, 3 to 4 rocket-throwers.

The mines and grenades that cannot be directly used in the Sahara should be reserved to supply the *wilayas* of the North.

But what is to be done with these weapons, in other words, how is the action to be carried out?

I see the thing in terms of two different directions: one vertical, the other horizontal.

The horizontal direction is the direction of supply, while the vertical is the direction of penetration.

Some forty individuals having a good knowledge of the Sahara and being first-rate militants could be appointed commando chiefs.

These commandos would operate in sections of 10. Each commando could be composed at the outset of 20 to 25 members, it being up to the chiefs to bring the number rapidly up to 100, even 150. Recruitment would be done locally at the outset.

Either Algerians living in Mali or Malian Touaregs themselves. This can be done in a month and a half. Between now and January 15th it is possible to arm and introduce into Algeria 500 to 800 armed men.

The first wave should be one of politicalization, mobilization. It should avoid encounters and let opportunities to strike the enemy slip by, even if success seems assured. Its role is to rouse the populations, to reassure them as to the future, to show the armament of the ALN, to detach them psychologically and mentally from enemy ascendancy.

In every sizeable tribe met up with, the commando must recruit three to four new members and leave three or four of its original members. The reason:

a) the new recruits know the terrain beyond, and at the beginning serve as a contact, as political interpreters, with the Northern tribes;

b) the members of the commando left on the spot prepare the various liaison channels that will receive the following waves.

One would then have the following pattern:

$\uparrow$ 80 to
$\downarrow$ 100 km.

11th base □ A □ B □ C □ D □ E □ F □ G □ H □ I □ J

$\uparrow$ 100 to
$\downarrow$ 150 km.

10th base □   □   □   □   □   □   □   □   □ □

9th base →

8th base →

7th base → (There would thus be a frontal position

6th base →   and a perpendicular direction.)

5th base →

4th base →

3rd base →

2nd base →

1st base →

0   base →

At the same time supply columns would be moving up to base 1.

Base 2 would send supply columns to base 1.

Base 3 to base 2 . . . and so forth. It is only when the advanced bases have received 3 or 4 shipments of supplies that the question of beginning operations can be considered.

At that time, moreover, contacts with the drivers and perhaps a better situation in the Fezzan will enable us to supply the ALN groups regularly.

Every group of 25 should have the following weaponry:

2 rocket-throwers and 20 shells;

2 machine guns, 1 of which should be anti-aircraft;

3 F.M.

The groups would leave at 2-day intervals. One radio sending station should be provided at the outset for base 0 located at D,

for the 4th base located at J,

for the 9th base located at A,

and 2 or 3 stations along the frontier.

These frontier stations would have listening-times in conjunction with the North General Staff and each of the stations of bases 0, 4 and 9.

2

Lumumba's Death:
Could We Do Otherwise?

Observers who happened to be in African capitals during the month of June 1960 could take note of a certain number of things. Strange personages who had come from a Congo which had just barely made its appearance on the international scene would turn up in ever greater numbers. What did these Congolese have to say? They said whatever came into their heads. That Lumumba had sold out to the Ghanaians. That Gizenga had been bought by the Guineans, Kashamura by the Yugoslavs. That the Belgian civilizers were leaving too soon, etc.

But if one took it into one's head to get one of these Congolese into a corner, to question him, then one discovered that something very serious was being plotted against Congo's independence and against Africa.

Congolese senators and deputies, immediately after the independence celebrations, would flee from the Congo and head for . . . the United States. Others would settle down for several weeks in Brazzaville. Trade unionists were invited to New York. Here, too, if one buttonholed one of these deputies or senators and questioned him, it became clear that a whole very precise procedure was about to be put into motion.

Already, before July 1st, 1960, the Katanga operation had been launched. Its objective? To safeguard the Union Minière, to be sure. But beyond this operation, it was Belgian interests that were being defended. A unified Congo, with a central government, went counter to Belgian interests. To support the slogans demanding the decentralization of the various provinces, to provoke these demands, to stir them into flame—such was the Belgian policy before independence.

The Belgians were aided in their task by the authorities of the Rhodesia-Nyasaland Federation. We know today, and Mr. Hammarskjöld knows it better than anyone, that before June 30, 1960, a Salisbury-Elizabethville airlift supplied Katanga with arms. Lumumba had once proclaimed that the liberation of the Congo would be the first phase of the complete independence of Central and Southern Africa and he had set his next objectives very precisely: support of the nationalist movements in Rhodesia, in Angola, in South Africa.

A unified Congo having at its head a militant anticolonialist constituted a real danger for South Africa, that very deep-South Africa before which the rest of the world veils its face. Or rather, before which the rest of the world is content to weep, as at Sharpeville, or to perform stylistic exercises on the occasion of anticolonialist day celebrations. Lumumba, because he was the chief of the first country in this region to obtain independence, because he knew concretely the weight of colonialism, had pledged in the name of his people to contribute physically to the death of that Africa. That the authorities of Katanga and those of Portugal have used every means to sabotage Congo's independence does not surprise us. That they have reinforced the action of the Belgians and increased the thrust of the centrifugal forces of the Congo is a fact. But this fact does not explain the deterioration that has progressively spread through the Congo; this fact does not explain the coldly planned, coldly executed murder of Lumumba. This colonialist collaboration is insufficient to explain why, in February 1961, Africa is about to experience its first great crisis over the Congo.

Africa's first great crisis, for she will have to decide whether to go forward or backward. She must understand that it is no longer possible to advance by regions, that, like a great body that refuses any mutilation, she must advance in totality, that there will not be one Africa that fights against colonialism and another that attempts to make arrangements with colonialism.

Africa, that is to say the Africans, must understand that there is never any greatness in procrastination and that there is never any dishonor in saying what one is and what one wants and that in reality the cleverness of the colonized can in the last analysis only be his courage, the lucid consciousness of his objectives and of his alliances, the tenacity that he brings to his liberation.

Lumumba believed in his mission. He had an exaggerated confidence in the people. The people, for him, not only could not deceive themselves but could not be deceived. And in fact everything seemed to prove him right. Every time, for example, that the enemies of the Congo succeeeded in arousing public opinion against him in a certain region, he only needed to appear, to explain, to denounce, for the situation again to become normal. He only forgot that he could not be everywhere at once and that the miracle of the explanation was less the truth of what he set forth than the truth of his person.

Lumumba had lost the battle for the presidency of the Republic. But because he embodied the confidence that the Congolese people had placed in him, because the African peoples had confusedly understood that he alone was concerned with the dignity of his country, Lumumba none the less continued to express Congolese patriotism and African nationalism in their most rigorous and noblest sense.

Then other countries much more important than Belgium or Portugal decided to take a direct interest in the question. Lumumba was contacted, questioned. After his trip to the United States the decision was reached: Lumumba must go.

Why? Because the enemies of Africa had understood. They had realized quite clearly that Lumumba was sold—sold to Africa, of course. In other words, he was no longer to be bought.

The enemies of Africa realized with a certain fear and trembling that if Lumumba should succeed, in the very heart of the colonialist empire, with a French Africa becoming transformed into a renovated community, an Angola as a "Portuguese province," and finally Eastern Africa, it was all up with "their" Africa, for which they had very precise plans.

The great success of the enemies of Africa is to have compromised the Africans themselves. It is true that these Africans were directly interested in the murder of Lumumba. Chiefs of puppet governments, in the midst of a puppet independence, facing day after day the wholesale opposition of their peoples, it did not take them long to convince themselves that the real independence of the Congo would put them personally in danger.

And there were other Africans, not altogether puppets, but who are frightened the moment the question of disengaging Africa from the West comes up. One has the impression that these African Chiefs of State are always afraid of facing Africa. They too, less actively, but consciously, have contributed to the deterioration of the situation in the Congo. Little by little, agreement was reached in the West that it was necessary to intervene in the Congo, that things could not be allowed to evolve at such a rate.

Little by little the idea of an intervention of the UN took shape. Then we can say today that two mistakes were simultaneously committed by the Africans.

First of all by Lumumba himself when he asked for the intervention of the UN. It was wrong to appeal to the UN. The UN has never been capable of validly settling a single one of the problems raised before the conscience of man by colonialism, and every time it has intervened, it was in order to come concretely to the rescue of the colonialist power of the oppressing country.

Look at Cameroon. What peace do Mr. Ahidjo's subjects enjoy, held in check by a French expeditionary force which, in large part, had its first fighting experience in Algeria? Yet the UN controlled the self-determination of Cameroon and the French government has set up a "provisional executive" there.

Look at Vietnam.

Look at Laos.

It is not true to say that the UN fails because the cases are difficult.

In reality the UN is the legal card used by the imperialist interests when the card of brute force has failed.

The partitions, the controlled joint commissions, the trustee-ship arrangements are international legal means of torturing, of crushing the will to independence of people, of cultivating anarchy, banditry, and wretchedness.

For after all, before the arrival of the UN, there were no massacres in the Congo. After the hallucinating rumors deliber-ately propagated in connection with the departure of the Belgians, only some ten dead were to be counted. But since the arrival of the UN we have grown used to learning every morn-ing that the Congolese were mutually massacring one another by the hundreds.

We are told today that the repeated provocations were cre-ated by Belgians disguised as soldiers of the United Nations. It is revealed to us today that civilian functionaries of the UN had in fact set up a new government on the third day of Lumumba's investiture. Now we understand much better what has been called Lumumba's violence, rigidity, and susceptibility.

Everything in fact shows that Lumumba was abnormally calm.

The heads of the UN mission made contact with Lumumba's enemies and with them made decisions by which the State of the Congo was committed. How should a head of government react in such a case? The aim sought and achieved is the following: to manifest the absence of authority, to prove the bankruptcy of the State.

In other words, to motivate the sequestering of the Congo.

Lumumba's mistake was then, in a first period, to believe in the UN's friendly impartiality. He forgot that the UN in its present state is only a reserve assembly, set up by the Great, to continue between two armed conflicts the "peaceful struggle" for the division of the world. If Mr. Ileo in August 1960 was telling anyone who would listen that Lumumba must be hanged, if the members of the Lumumba cabinet did not know what to do with the dollars which, at this period, began to invade Leopoldville, and finally if Mobutu went every evening to Brazzaville to do and hear what we can more readily guess today, why then turn with such sincerity, such absence of reserve, to the UN?

Africans must remember this lesson. If we need outside aid, let us call our friends. They alone can really and totally help us achieve our objectives because, precisely, the friendship that links us is a friendship of combat.

But the African countries for their part committed a mistake by their willingness to send their troops under the cover of the UN. In fact they were permitting themselves to be neutralized and, without suspecting it, they were allowing others to do their work.

They should have sent troops to Lumumba, to be sure, but not within the framework of the UN. Directly. From one friendly country to another friendly country. The African troops in the Congo have suffered a historic moral defeat. With arms at the ready, they watched without reacting (because they were UN troops) the disintegration of a State and a nation that all Africa had saluted and sung. A shame.

Our mistake, the mistake we Africans made, was to have forgotten that the enemy never withdraws sincerely. He never understands. He capitulates, but he does not become converted.

Our mistake is to have believed that the enemy had lost his combativeness and his harmfulness. If Lumumba is in the way, Lumumba disappears. Hesitation in murder has never characterized imperialism.

Look at Ben M'hidi, look at Moumié, look at Lumumba. Our mistake is to have been slightly confused in what we did. It is a fact that in Africa, today, traitors exist. They should have been denounced and fought. The fact that this is hard after the magnificent dream of an Africa gathered together unto itself and subject to the same requirements of true independence does not alter facts.

Africans have endorsed the imperialist police in the Congo, have served as intermediaries, have sponsored the activities and the odd silences of the UN in the Congo.

Today they are afraid. They vie with one another in shedding crocodile tears round the tomb of Lumumba. Let us not be fooled; they are expressing the fear of their principals. The imperialists too are afraid. And they are right, for many Africans, many Afro-Asiatics have understood. The imperialists are going to pause for a while. They are going to wait for "the righteous indignation" to calm. We must take advantage of this brief respite to abandon our fearful approaches and decide to save the Congo and Africa.

The imperialists decided to do away with Lumumba. They have done so. They decided to raise legions of volunteers. These are already on the spot.

The Katanga air force, under orders from South African and Belgian pilots, has in the last few days begun machine gunning on the ground. From Brazzaville, foreign planes arrive crowded with volunteers and parachute officers who have come to the rescue of a certain Congo.

If we decide to support Gizenga, we must do so resolutely.

For no one knows the name of the next Lumumba. There is in Africa a certain tendency represented by certain men. It is this tendency, dangerous for imperialism, which is at issue. Let us be sure never to forget it: the fate of all of us is at stake in the Congo.